WHO WAS EDGAR CAYCE?

EDGAR CAYCE, unwitting seer and clairvoyant, touched millions of lives with his innate spiritual wisdom and his uncanny healing visions.

Born in 1877 in Hopkinsville, Kentucky, Edgar Cayce had a seventh-grade education, yet was able to repeat complex and technical medical jargon when under a trance. In this state, he was said to heal many of the people who came seeking his counsel with his recommendations for medical treatment. Cayce soon began to talk about spiritual notions such as Atlantis, reincarnation, dreams, astrology, and more. He would also predict some of the more astounding events of the twentieth century, such as World Wars and the Great Depression.

The Washington Post wrote: "His words have inspired faith in spirituality, which for many people is more powerful than science." Called the "sleeping prophet" and "America's greatest psychic," Cayce, who died in 1945, may have been the first to usher in what is now known as the New Age Movement. More than fifty years after his death, his work continues to influence our lives in powerful new ways.

DEATH
DOES NOT
PART US

DEATH DOES NOT PART US

ELSIE R. SECHRIST

St. Martin's Paperbacks

Published by arrangement with A.R.E. Press.

DEATH DOES NOT PART US

Library of Congress Catalog Card Number: 92-27513

ISBN: 0-312-96901-5

Printed in the United States of America

A.R.E. Press edition/May 1995
St. Martin's Paperbacks edition/April 1999

St. Martin's Paperbacks are published by St. Martin's Press, 175 Fifth Avenue, New York, NY 10010.

10 9 8 7 6 5 4 3 2 1

CONTENTS

When a soul goes through the birth process, the angels in heaven do weep, while those on earth rejoice. When a soul goes through the death process, the family on earth does weep, while the angels in heaven rejoice.

For those who believe, no proof is necessary. For those who do not believe, no proof is possible.

DEDICATIONS

THIS BOOK IS lovingly and humbly dedicated to two men who have played such a valuable role in my life.

First, I dedicate this volume to Edgar Cayce, better known as the "sleeping prophet of Virginia Beach." There have been dozens of books written about him and his work. Several million copies later, there is little that can be added. Mr. Cayce possessed a most unusual psychic gift which he used, for almost his entire adult life, to serve humankind. Through discourses that he called "readings," he gave the information, obtained through his psychic perception, to people with health problems and to those with questions regarding every aspect of life and living, as well as death and religious philosophies.

It was my very good fortune to know this man and to receive psychic advice from him. His guidance was of immense help to me physically, mentally, and spiritually.

Today, nearly fifty years later, Edgar Cayce is still "about his Father's business," even though he has passed on. He is still giving advice and help to souls on this side of life—and on that other side as well. He is aiding them in understanding and coping with existence in both our world and the afterlife.

I also want my deceased husband, Bill, to share in this dedication; for it was he who made my life worthwhile!

FOREWORD

ELSIE SECHRIST AND her husband, Bill, met Edgar Cayce in January 1943. They were close personal friends until Mr. Cayce's death in 1945. During that time they both received psychic readings from this ''sleeping prophet''—guidance that changed the course of their lives.

Mrs. Sechrist quickly began what was to become the major interest in her life: the development of ''A Search for God'' study groups. They are small groups that meet weekly in hundreds of communities throughout North America and dozens of countries worldwide. Spiritual assistance is the purpose of these groups, which she supported so wholeheartedly. They provide a framework where people can study and then test in their own lives the helpful ideas available from the Cayce readings regarding each soul's quest for oneness with God. This help can come especially through prayer, meditation, and dreams—subjects about which Mrs. Sechrist has knowledgeably explored in her books, *Meditation-Gateway to Light* and *Dreams-Your Magic Mirror*. In nearly four decades of active work, she and her husband helped to organize countless ''A Search for God'' groups and provided the needed inspiration for untold thousands of people to join in this activity.

In those early years of the Association for Research and Enlightenment, just before and after Edgar Cayce's death, Mrs. Sechrist and a handful of other dedicated workers provided the strong base from which three current organizations now operate: the A.R.E., the Edgar Cayce Foundation, and Atlantic University. For many years Elsie and Bill Sechrist served as International Representatives of the A.R.E. They spent much of each year lecturing and conducting seminars overseas in dozens of countries, in addition to their travels throughout America. Mrs. Sechrist was known world-wide as a captivating teacher and seminar leader at colleges, universities, churches, and A.R.E. conferences.

One special interest of Elsie's was working within church communities to incorporate many of the spiritual ideas she had learned from the Cayce readings. She felt that our churches are real assets and that we should do all we can to support them and make them an even more vital place for spiritual growth.

The death of Bill in 1987 and of Elsie on April 12, 1992, were deep losses to our organization. But we trust that their invaluable efforts with this work continue on the other side of life as well.

This book about vivid evidence of life after death is a fitting last installment in Mrs. Sechrist's extraordinary legacy to all spiritual seekers. To any friend or relative with questions about death, this is the book I would recommend because its inspiring stories answer the concerns we all carry about the afterlife. It's a unique compilation of visions and unusual dream accounts—a tapestry of experiences which weaves a vivid and hopeful picture about life after death.

Mrs. Sechrist made an extensive study of the Cayce readings on this subject, in addition to forty years of research and investigation across the broad field of parapsychology. What is most impressive, she conferred with thousands of individuals from all walks of life regarding their paranormal experiences. In creating this volume, she collected written accounts from people around the world who had firsthand experiences suggesting that the soul survives physical death. Taken as a whole, these accounts are powerful evidence for the continuity of life *and* hopeful insights about what we can expect on the other side.

As president of the A.R.E., when I reflect on the work of my grandfather Edgar Cayce and this organization's history, I'm not sure where we would be without the efforts of Elsie and Bill Sechrist. All of us who have benefited from the Cayce readings thank them for their contributions to this work. More important, tens of thousands of us have been helped through Mrs. Sechrist's teaching and writing. I'm sure that countless more will be helped by this book, her final gift to us before moving on to the new life that it so beautifully describes.

Charles Thomas Cayce, Ph.D.
President
Association for Research and Enlightenment, Inc.

PREFACE

FOR ALMOST FIFTY years I have been interested in and have sought to understand men's and women's rather short span of life here on earth. At the same time, I have tried to establish conclusive evidence for survival of the soul after physical death.

I was fortunate beyond words in that shortly after I began my studies and research, I met Edgar Cayce, the "sleeping prophet." There was an instantaneous rapport between us, occasioned by past lives together, according to the psychic information Cayce later gave to me. It was an association that began in Egypt 12,000 years ago. Our working together continued during later incarnations in ancient Egypt and Persia, in the Holy Land, and in modern-day America.

During most of his adult life, Mr. Cayce regularly set aside a time to go into a trancelike state, in which he laid aside the identification with the physical body and conscious mind. This state enabled him to contact deeper levels of his being and thus to receive information beyond that of which he was consciously aware. This material was communicated in a number of discourses, known as "readings." Over 14,000 readings were stenographically recorded and have been preserved to the present, available to anyone who wants to explore his fascinating ideas. Each of Cayce's readings was assigned a two-part number. The first number identified the individual for whom the reading was given; this was used to insure the privacy of the individual. The second number indicated the serial number of the reading for the particular individual. Thus, reading 5330-1 means that this information was contained in the first reading given for the person who was assigned the number 5330.

Edgar Cayce's discourses cover a vast range of subjects. Two of the largest categories are the physical readings (which diagnosed health problems and recommended natural, holistic treatments) and the life readings (which traced the development of the individual soul through its earlier incarnations and on into the present). Other readings provided business advice, dream interpretations, or mental and spiritual guidance. And a number of discourses were given to help groups of people work toward specific goals they had chosen to pursue together. The study group series of readings, which formed the basis of the "Search for God" material, is a prime example of such readings.

Though I received personal psychic discourses, or "readings," from Cayce, my greatest blessing came through the numerous hours we spent together in intense conversation. His patience in answering my questions was limitless. Many times his responses were followed by vignettes illustrating his personal philosophy or experience. His answers were profound. Regrettably, our association this time around came only during the last few years of his life. I was, however, further privileged in having the opportunity to study at my leisure all of the readings.

My personal association with Cayce, coupled with my in-depth study of his readings, gave me the answers for which I was searching. The result is such an intermingling of information, coming both from the waking Cayce and from his readings, that I find it impossible to separate what he revealed to me firsthand from what is written in his readings. This is of no consequence because to me the source was the same.

The view of life and death Cayce proposed, through

both his conscious thoughts and his psychic discourses, is at once helpful, hopeful, and consistent. It is based upon an uncomplicated, secure foundation. The first premise or fact is that God exists. We recognize that all of nature, all heaven and earth, declares this simple truth. The Creator of heaven and earth and all that they hold IS! From this starting point, the following philosophy is spelled out carefully in the Cayce readings—a philosophy which, I believe, is convincingly supported by the material I present in this book.

Each human being is a portion of God, created by Him and out of Him. So there is within each of us that imperishable part that is divine. Being divine, this part of us can never die. It may lie unconscious or asleep within us for a long time—as we measure time—but it can never be lost or destroyed.

Within each of our minds is the consciousness of this divine element, which is our essence. The Cayce readings refer to this awareness of the Divine within as the *Christ Consciousness*. This consciousness of the God within us makes each soul aware of its relationship with the creative force.

In this way, the human mind partakes of the spiritual realm. But mind is material, too. In comparing the trinity of our own make-up (body, mind, and spirit) to the Holy Trinity (Father, Son, and Holy Spirit), Cayce suggests a close link between the mind and the Christ. The mind can play a role like the Christ, the Word of God; and this Word can be made manifest in materiality. Christ dwelt among people who beheld His face as that of the Father! We have Jesus' own promise of this oneness with the Divine: ". . . he that hath seen me hath seen the Father . . ." (John 14:9) Through His life we were shown the glory of God on earth.

All nature declares and expresses the glory of its Creator. Can we humans do less? The glory of God abides in love, for God is love. The purpose of each soul's entering into life is to manifest more and more the love of God for all humanity. We can express our own divinity only through the way in which we treat others.

According to Edgar Cayce, God has granted us not just one chance to manifest our divinity in this way; each of us is given, through reincarnation, many such chances. This, the possibility to show forth the love of God to those around us, is the opportunity presented to each soul in every lifetime. The soul enters physical life through its own choice. Every experience we come into is but one of a series of lifetimes, each one being the result of what we have done in the past with the knowledge and resources available to us. In evaluating our progress, we can ask ourselves, "Are my deeds improving the quality of my life so that I become more helpful and constructive with all whom I meet?" If so, we can know that we are using our opportunities in physical life to fulfill our potential as children of God by expressing His love for others.

Only our sins separate us, temporarily, from being one with our Creator. Edgar Cayce said that if, over the course of eons and innumerable lifetimes, a soul refuses to follow its divine self, then that soul can lose its personal identity. It will be reabsorbed into the Creative Energy of Life, or God, as a drop of water is reunited with the sea. But the readings indicate that drastic conclusion would be rare. The more usual course is for the soul, through its experiences in physical life and the afterlife, to grow toward a recognition of its relationship with God. Again, our understanding of this divine companionship is shown in our actions and attitudes toward other people. As our realization of our relationship with God becomes clearer, we become more and more aware of His guidance, His voice, which speaks to us through the voice of our own conscience.

This spiritual development is a unified process of growth, resulting from the soul's experience on *both sides* of the change we know as death. To be absent from the body—physically dead—is to be present with that consciousness that has been our ideal, our God. It is a spiritual law, not always realized, that the manner in which we treat our fellow human beings is the way we are treating our Father and our God. So, our actions toward others affect the consciousness we will experience after death.

We know that the one great law is to "love the Lord thy God with all thy heart, and with all thy soul, and with all thy strength, and with all thy mind; and thy neighbor as thyself." (Luke 10:27) Here is the measuring rod for all humanity. This law embodies the criteria for each soul's experience, by which its sincerity of purpose and desire can be judged. This, as the Scriptures tell us, is the whole law. As we bring our entire existence into accord with this law, we come to know the truth of Jesus' promise, "Ye abide in me, as I in the Father . . . and I will come and abide with thee." (John 14:20, 23) All the soul's experiences, in this world and the next, have the purpose of leading us into this complete realization of divine love.

With this in mind, what are we to believe when a loved one dies? What are we to feel? Rather than giving in to a sense of hopelessness, we can recognize that God has given us an avenue of escape from this plane. He has given us another opportunity in another world—that plane of consciousness known as the afterlife—in which we can broaden our understanding. Edgar Cayce pointed out in his psychic readings that it is through that which we call death that we really experience God's love. As we stated earlier in a slightly different way, to be absent from the body is to be present with that which the soul has worshiped.

The Bible tells us that we are created to become companions with God. But flesh and blood may not inherit eternal life. Only the spirit, the purpose, the desire may claim this inheritance. The body, created by our God, is but the vehicle for the soul's expression in the earth. It is not the part of us that can achieve everlasting union with our Creator. It is necessary for the physical to pass away, so that the divine portion of the soul can advance into eternal life in God, which has been our promise from the beginning.

All of the foregoing is a statement of spiritual philosophy that I have adopted from my many years of studying and applying the Cayce readings. It has established in my mind the unshakable conviction that *we are forever*, whether in this life on earth or in the soul's existence across the threshold of that called death. This book is written to present the evidence, the substantiation, for that conviction. It is based upon my own convincing experiences, those of my correspondents around the world, and others related to me by Edgar Cayce.

My focus is different from the many recent research reports and books dealing with only near-death experiences. Those publications, clearly of much value, deal almost exclusively with the process of dying. They examine the transition and moments just after death. Although my book examines those elements, in addition I try to go a step or two beyond the transition itself, into an investigation of what awaits us in the afterlife. The material collected here provides a number of fascinating details about existence on the other side of life, as well as persuasive grounds for belief in the immortality of the soul.

Elsie Sechrist
January 1992

GOD'S OTHER CHAMBER

"**FOR THERE IS** not death, to those who love the Lord; only the entering into God's other chamber." (Edgar Cayce reading 2282-1)

Many years ago a true story, written by Taylor Caldwell, appeared in *The American Weekly*. Entitled "Joy's Christmas Miracle," this account convincingly illustrates that we survive the death of the body.

The story tells of a woman whose husband, Carl, was a reserve officer in the United States Army. He was called into service in Korea. Within six months' time, Carl was killed in action, leaving his wife and their seven-year-old son, Skip. With no other family to support her, the woman was practically alone with her child.

She and her husband had each been reared in a very materialistic way. At the time of Carl's death, she could not name even one of the Ten Commandments. Their son, too, had been raised without any of those old-fashioned beliefs in God.

As a result of her philosophy, the woman was devastated at her husband's death. She felt there was no such thing as meeting him on the other side of that barrier, either in her dreams or in another life. For her, except for the child, life was over, and her husband no longer existed—anywhere. She was beside herself with grief, completely without hope.

Skip had just passed his eighth birthday when he began complaining of headaches. Examination by experts showed that the boy was suffering from a brain tumor. An operation told the story. Skip had cancer of the brain and had only a few months to live.

Imagine the mother's anguish! Every day she read to her darling son and sang songs for him. Every day he grew weaker and his sight grew dimmer. Finally his legs were paralyzed and he began to sink into unconsciousness. Pain-killing drugs eased his suffering, but unconsciousness was quickly taking over.

Christmas Eve came. The tree was aglow with lights, and gifts lay around it. But Skip could not even see them. For perhaps the first time in her life, his mother began to pray—agonizingly and tearfully.

Then she heard footsteps. Thinking it was the night nurse, she started to say, "You shouldn't have come tonight." But at that point Skip cried out, "Daddy, Daddy! Look, Mommy, Daddy's come home!"

The woman looked up and saw Carl in all his youthful splendor, standing there and smiling. She was speechless. Her husband spoke: "It's all right, my love. I've come home tonight to see you and Skip and to tell you there is a devoted Father who truly loves us all. He sent me to help you and Skip."

Skip sat up in bed and pointed to the tree. "Look, Daddy, the tree! Isn't it beautiful?"

The father gazed at the tree and the star on top, and he said softly, "It is beautiful. And the star on top of the tree is the star of our life, Skip."

The mother watched her dearly beloved husband as he gently pushed their son back on his pillows, urging him to go to sleep so he could open his gifts the next day. He told the boy that he would soon be well and back in school. Within a month Skip was well, his sight was restored, and his legs were strong. Examinations showed the child to be cured! Specialists came from far and near to hear the story and to report on it.

Skip was a healthy teen-ager when this report appeared. The account of his family's experience holds a powerful message of hope that can benefit all of us. For death—our own or that of a loved one—is something each of us must face. This can be a dismal prospect if the physical body is considered to be all that we are, and death the absolute end of our existence.

But the return of Skip's father shows that we do have a life beyond the body. There is something vital within us that is overlooked by the materialistic viewpoint the family held during the first part of this story. This is the message that Carl brought through his visit, and Skip's subsequent recovery offers proof that the experience was valid. We do survive death, to reunite with our loving God. Indeed it is true, there is no death of the soul.

During the course of my study of physical death, I have received accounts from numerous correspondents around the world. Like the story related above, each of these experiences provides evidence that part of us survives the demise of the body. Throughout this material there is the assurance that the separation we know as death is not final.

I myself have had several convincing experiences which demonstrated that those who pass from this earth do not cease to exist. In one instance, this basic truth was impressed on me by the loveliness and compassion of the soul who communicated with me and by the relevance of the information she gave. Through this happening, I personally received clear confirmation that the deceased not only continue to live, they continue to be aware of us and to care.

The story begins while I was living in Los Angeles and had the opportunity to start a group which met weekly to study the contents of two books entitled *A Search for God.* This material was the result of the work done by some of Edgar Cayce's closest followers.

At our first meeting, in Beverly Hills, I was struck by the sadness of Florence, our hostess. After the meeting I asked one of her friends why she looked so sad. I learned that her very best friend, whom she adored, had just passed on. That night I prayed for Florence. As I did so, a woman with the most beautiful and sympathetic blue eyes approached me in a vision and said, "I am Florence's friend. Would you please give her these three messages?" She then told me the three items she wanted me to convey to Florence.

The next morning I called Florence, described her friend—particularly her eyes—and relayed the three messages. I heard a gasp, almost a cry, as she said, "It was she! Everyone always talks about her beautiful, compassionate eyes."

Then she said, "And do you know, those three messages she gave you for me are answers to questions my husband and I discussed this very morning? Now I know there is no death, and my friend is alive—somewhere!"

In my attempt to understand life and death, I have been greatly aided by information received from Edgar Cayce. His material furnishes much insight into our nature and our experiences in physical life and beyond. A number of readings give us a sense of the close relationship between life and death, and the serenity that accepting this relationship can bring. For example, he told one person in a reading: ". . . it is not all of life to live, nor yet all of death to die. For life and death are one, and only those who will consider the experience as one may come to understand or comprehend what peace indeed means." (1977-1)

Aside from giving readings, Edgar Cayce had several other experiences in which the gap between physical life and death was, for a time, bridged. One has clearly stayed in my memory. He once told my husband Bill and me of the following incident, which illustrated the continuity of existence, personality, and awareness after death.

Mr. Cayce and a friend had been arguing about survival of the soul. Cayce believed in it, his friend did not. To resolve the question, they made a pact that whichever of them died first, that one would attempt to come back and prove survival.

Some time later, the friend died.

Late one evening after the death, Mr. Cayce was at home listening to the "Seth Parker Program" on his radio. Suddenly he clairvoyantly saw his deceased friend sitting in a large chair across from him.

His friend said, "Cayce, you are right! There is survival of personality."

With that the room was filled with unseen people, who began to sing. Cayce was so unnerved that he ran upstairs and jumped into bed.

When he got there, his wife Gertrude said, "Edgar, you have forgotten to turn off the radio."

Mr. Cayce said, "No, I didn't, and I'm not about to go down and see."

Apparently the chorus of people and voices continued for a while, even after he had gone to bed.

On another occasion, Mr. Cayce had an experience in which he was shown a very detailed picture of the transition from life to death. This incident, told to me by Hugh Lynn Cayce, Edgar Cayce's elder son, illustrates the range of information that was available to Cayce while he was in trance. It also shows that an approaching death can be foreseen; it doesn't just happen randomly, on the spur of the moment.

One time, after giving a reading in his psychic state, Edgar Cayce failed to follow the usual suggestion for him to regain normal, waking consciousness. Instead he said, speaking to himself, "If you, Edgar Cayce, want to see your mother alive once more, you had better visit her immediately!"

After awakening and being told of this message, Cayce at once bought a ticket to his home in Hopkinsville, Kentucky. When he got there, his mother seemed completely well! He did not tell her why he had come unannounced. The next day, however, she went to bed, feeling ill. While she did not appear to be suffering very much, her son nonetheless sat with her for two days. Her only complaint at that time was a general weakness.

During this period Edgar Cayce, with his inner perception, observed her soul moving into and out of her physical body. He saw his deceased grandparents' arrival on the scene, and he watched as they spoke with their child, his mother. After her conversation with her parents, she—her soul—re-entered the physical body and she again talked with her son. She told him that on the next day her parents would come for her and she would go with them.

The following day Edgar Cayce watched the loved ones reunite. There is indeed no death—merely a transition.

There are several remarkable features to this experience of Edgar Cayce and his mother, and I'll refer to this story several times in later chapters. But one feature especially stands out: the peacefulness of the transition. As seen here, what waits for us beyond death is in no way fearsome. Perhaps this is only to be expected in Mrs. Cayce's instance, since the circumstances of her death were practically ideal for a gentle passage. She had the opportunity to make her change gradually and without extreme pain. Several of her loved ones were with her physically at the time of her demise, and other souls dear to her waited to receive her on the other side.

Our next story, however, describes a far different manner of death.

A MURDERED GIRL LOVES HEAVEN

The following is a true account about a fourteen-year-old girl who had been murdered. Her story was the subject of an article entitled ''Awaiting Justice,'' which appeared in the *Houston Chronicle*.

The *Chronicle* report relates a dream of the victim's mother, in which she was visited by her deceased daughter, Carolyn. The girl told her mother what had happened and described her killer, who had not yet been identified at the time the story appeared. The girl said that he was someone she did not know.

Apparently the crime occurred after Carolyn had gone swimming in the apartment-house pool. She had returned to the family apartment after her swim and had been killed there. In the dream, she told her mother that she had fought off the man as best she could. The blood-splattered room indicated that a struggle had indeed taken place. A butcher knife, found in a kitchen drawer, was the murder weapon; although it had been washed, it still had some blood on it. Robbery was evidently the motive for the crime, since money and jewelry were missing, and examination proved that the girl had not been raped. Police have yet to find the murderer.

It seems that the reason Carolyn appeared in her mother's dream was to offer consolation. Her eyes, large and gray-blue, were full of compassion. She seemed very happy in the dream, and she told her mother that she loved heaven. She asked her not to worry and urged her to try to forget the manner of her death. Apparently, we who are left behind suffer far more at the loss of a dear soul than does the individual who has departed.

Carolyn's violent end contrasts strongly with Mrs. Cayce's death. We can well imagine that the circumstances of Carolyn's demise were fearful, and the transition itself an extremely traumatic event. Yet this story shows that even though the events surrounding death may be terrifying, the soul can still pass into a state of happiness. It is not necessary to die peacefully, as Edgar Cayce's mother did, in order to discover peace beyond. This knowledge can be a source of great comfort to any of us with loved ones who have met death suddenly and violently.

It might seem to some that the experience of Caro-

lyn's mother could be written off as "just a dream."
But the Cayce readings tell us that the messages we receive through our dreams are often quite valid. They
come "for the benefit of the individual, [if we would]
but interpret them correctly . . ." (294-15) Through the
years Cayce gave hundreds of dream-interpretation readings. This material shows dreams to be an important
source of information, fresh perspectives, and understanding. In some cases, dreams offer foreknowledge of
events to come or views into the life beyond.

Many of the reports from my correspondents tell of
dream contacts with the deceased. These accounts are
quite similar to ones Edgar Cayce was asked to comment
on during his lifetime. In a good number of instances,
he confirmed that such dream encounters were *actual
communication* with the souls of the dead, rather than
just the result of wishful thinking on the part of the
dreamer. In a reading for a young woman who sensed
the presence of her departed mother in her dreams,
Cayce offered reassurance that we can be visited by deceased loved ones as we sleep. In response to her concern that these extraordinary dreams were a trick her
mind was playing on her, Cayce said, "No, not fooling
self, for the *soul* liveth, and is at peace, and would [have
you] know that it liveth." (136–33)

This promise gives us a sense of the abundant comfort we can find in the enduring presence of those who
have been dear to us in life. Our next story illustrates
the very real, very powerful effect this consolation can
have. The peace and joy brought to our narrator by her
deceased husband's visit, and the feeling that the same
peace and joy are part of his experience after death, offer
encouragement to any of us faced with the departure of
a loved one.

A DEVOTED COMPANION
RECONFIRMS HIS LOVE

In this story, which presents a vivid picture of the survival of love beyond the grave, our contributor describes her first visit from her departed husband. (Her three later contacts with her spouse are related in Chapter 6.)

"My story is about paranormal experiences with my deceased husband, Artie. I've had four such experiences. I know they are real and valid, and they have meant so much to me. I've discovered that other people are very reluctant to discuss such events. I wonder why.

"Many, many nights before his death, my husband and I sat and talked with each other, either outdoors or in the house. We discussed so many things—life, death, and life after death. It was a wonderful time of the day for us, examining and exchanging ideas.

"I have always read a great deal and loved to explore fresh thoughts with others. I have an enormous need for new knowledge and an insatiable curiosity about life, God, the universe, and all that affects us as human beings. Artie neither read nor talked a great deal; he was, however, a good listener, and he was interested in what I was learning—but he certainly didn't always agree!

"Through our discussions, we had pretty much come to the conclusion that our lives do not end with death, but continue on somewhere not too different from this earth. After death our souls would, of course, have a type of body in order to retain the consciousness, love, knowledge, and abilities we had developed.

"My husband died at six o'clock on the Saturday morning of a holiday weekend, two days after having been admitted to the hospital with a mild heart attack. Strangely enough, our son had called Friday night to say he was flying in to see his father on Saturday morning. I told him his dad was feeling better and had taken some solid food the day before, but he said he wanted to come anyway. The next morning, Artie passed on.

"Shortly after his funeral, I had the following experience: Our dog had always slept at the foot of our bed; but every night since Artie's death, she had gotten up onto his side of the bed. I would stretch out my legs and push her off.

"On Friday night a week after Artie had died, just as I was going to sleep, I thought the dog was trying to get on the bed again. I was about to push her off with my foot, when I had the feeling it wasn't the dog. I said, 'Artie?' and I felt him lie down beside me! He put his arms around me and laid his head on my shoulder. I was filled with an indescribable peace such as I had never experienced before.

"Artie then said, 'Yes, I remember all the things I was and knew and felt. Yes, I am fine and will go on being me, learning and building my life. Yes, I will be here and waiting for you when you come.' I didn't ask anything. I didn't even try to see him. It was enough to know he was O.K. somewhere, so I simply went peacefully to sleep. But what a wonderful thing to have happened and what a beautiful reaffirmation of our philosophy! Strangely enough, too, the dog never tried to get up on the bed again. She loved him so! Perhaps he had reassured her in some way, too.

"Later, when I told the children about this experience, their reactions were interesting, of course. The girls didn't say very much, although they were moved. It is hard to know how to respond to something as unexpected as this. One of them said later that she thought it was a dream. But I know that nothing so real and comforting and substantial could be a dream. It really happened! I really felt him and in my mind I knew his thoughts.

"I think one of my other daughters' comments hit

the nail on the head when she said, 'Wasn't it just like Daddy to do that—to reassure Mother so?' And indeed it was."   *M. A.*

This story, like the bulk of my correspondence, shows that death is not something to be feared. Truly, there can be difficulties after death, just as there are before. There is a continuity between life and death. When we make the transition, we lose neither our existence nor our identity. Death—as the Cayce readings spoke of it—is only "passing through God's other door." (1472-2) This continuity can work both ways. Generally, knowledge of our continuation is a source of comfort to us. But just as a person can get stuck in unproductive behavior before death, the same can happen to a soul on the other side. Our next story shows us one example of such a problem.

THE SOUL WHO NEEDED A PUSH

My husband Bill and I had a remarkable experience while on a speaking tour in Europe. We were giving a public lecture in Paris in November 1985. After the lecture, a young woman came up to ask a question. I saw that she was wearing Saint Catherine Labouré's Miraculous Medal. The unembalmed yet perfectly preserved body of "The Saint of Silence," Saint Catherine, lies in a glass case on the altar of La Chappelle, located at 140 Rue du Boc in Paris, France. Many miracles were attributed to this saint during her lifetime. Many more have occurred since her death.

Since this particular medal is not too common, I asked her why she was wearing it. She did not know the history of the saint, but proceeded to tell us her own story. Her uncle had died about three years earlier. Almost immediately after his death, he began to bother her—both during her dreams and in her waking state.

She implied that there were sexual overtones.

This annoyance became so disturbing that she spoke to her confessor about it. The priest was unable to help the woman himself, but he suggested that she go to La Chappelle and arrange for Masses to be offered up for her uncle. She followed this recommendation and, at once, her uncle ceased bothering her. At the time she spoke with us, more than a year had passed without incident. It is obvious that through the prayers which were offered, the uncle received the message and moved on his way of advancement and enlightenment.

Although this report shows that souls can run into difficulties after death, it also holds out hope. It illustrates that the problems of the dead, like those of the living, have solutions. We are not mired in one experience forever after our demise. The idea of eternal damnation is not supported by the Edgar Cayce material, by the stories my respondents have sent me, nor by my own experiences with those who have passed on. Any difficulties encountered by the soul after death can be dealt with and overcome.

Often these difficulties are met with assistance from the living. The dead not only continue to exist; they continue to be aware of us. Thus, our activities can affect them and help them. Our opportunity to express love for those close to us does not end with their death. Sometimes the solution comes about through prayer, a frequent theme in the stories I have collected. Praying for the dead is an extremely powerful way to help them continue their development.

A final story of this chapter wonderfully illustrates many of the ideas we've met so far: The dead continue to live; generally, their condition is one of contentment and peace; they continue to love us and be responsive to us; and through contact with them we can receive a great deal of comfort and consolation.

CONSOLATION FROM A DEPARTED SON

The following account, remarkable for the sense of reality it conveys, was sent to me by a woman whose son had passed on at a very young age:

"Following the death of Eric, my son, I dreamed that I moved from the home where I had raised my children. I was concerned that now Eric had no place in which to sleep, and I told him so. He stood before me, placed his hand on the bedroom furniture—the bed on which he had been conceived and had later died—and said, 'Don't worry, Mommy. I have a place to sleep.' This, to me, was reassurance that he was O.K. and was in a state of rest at that moment.

"Some time later, in a 'dream,' I received a special gift from God. I had, in my sorrow, wished that I could hold and kiss my deceased son just one more time. In this experience—more like a vision than an ordinary dream—I seemed to be groping about in the darkness, my eyes sealed tightly shut. Suddenly, someone gently reached out to me from behind and turned me around. It was Eric! He drew me into his arms and kissed and hugged me. I could feel his body in my arms, right down to the bones and muscles in his shoulders.

"I felt his hair on my cheek. As I buried my face in his shoulder, I could even smell the 'just washed' fabric of his favorite 'rock' tee shirt and feel the texture of it on my face. It was wonderful, and the feeling was too real not to be valid.

"As I awoke I could still feel my arms full of him; and then, too quickly, it faded as I came back to the conscious world. I was so happy that the Lord had let me hold my baby one more time, as I had wished. Although the moment was too brief, I had that moment. Eric came back to tell me that he loves me and that he is alive, as full of life as when I felt him in my arms during my 'dream' experience.

"Well, Elsie, that's what has happened to me to date. I know right now that my deep sorrow sometimes makes me a poor channel to receive my son's messages, but I'm trying to recover. I hope there will be more to tell you later."

M. H.

2

DEATH AND RE-BIRTH

IT IS ONLY natural when a loved one dies to wish he or she could come back to physical life again. Even though death is an irreversible process from a material standpoint, evidence suggests that our natural wish is not so far-fetched. Not only will we be reunited with loved ones in the afterlife, the Cayce readings (and many other spiritual teachings) indicate that we can look forward to experiences together again in the physical world.

This is the ancient concept of reincarnation, a theory of re-birth that puts death and dying into a very different context than the one that governs our mainstream, Western mind-set. The following story is a good example of how one woman, who was open to the theory of reincarnation, was able to understand a psychic contact with a little boy who had passed on. She had enjoyed a special closeness with her very appealing nephew. Her account conveys the uplifting message that rewarding relationships like theirs need not end with death.

A JOYFUL REUNION

''I can recall two incidents in which I was visited by close relatives following their physical deaths. The first contact was with a nephew, Toby; the second, with my father. Both contacts occurred at night while I was sleeping. The experiences weren't visual so much as auditory.

I couldn't actually see either of my visitors, but I felt their presence and knew that they were talking to me.

"My nephew Toby was just over three years old when he died. He had been born with multiple heart problems. The day before he died he was operated on for the third time. Although the surgery was a success, Toby's body didn't adjust to the stress, and he had a heart attack. Before I describe his visit from the other side, I'd like to tell you a little about Toby.

"Toby was a beautiful child—platinum curls, a round cherubic face, and powder blue eyes. In spite of his illness, he was the most joyful being I've ever encountered. No one who saw him was untouched by the absolute love he generated and gave. Toby was my sister's first child and the second grandchild in the family. My sister had had a very difficult labor and delivery, and she and Toby were kept in the hospital for a week after his birth.

"The first time I saw Toby, he was about two weeks old. From that moment forward I knew he was a special gift and would not be with us long. The very fact that he survived birth and lived for three months without medical help attested to his will to live. He was continually in pain, he couldn't breathe while sucking a bottle, and his heart was incredibly damaged; but even so, he was full of life. His little eyes just sparkled, sending flames across the room, gathering all to him.

"I spent a lot of time with Toby and my sister during those three short years of his life. After he died, my sister and her husband moved to another part of the state, and they have since had two beautiful, healthy children.

"Toby came to me on December 6, the anniversary of his death, after my sister had delivered her second son in April. He kept insistently calling for 'Aunt Linda, Aunt Linda,' until I became lucid. I remember thinking it couldn't be Jonathan, my sister's new son, because he couldn't talk yet. When I realized it was Toby, he told me, 'Don't be sad, Aunt Linda. I'm coming back! I'm coming back!' He was so happy, and I was elated.

"That morning at five o'clock, my best friend called to tell me she had given birth to a baby girl at around 3:00 a.m. As nearly as I can figure, that was about the time Toby had come to see me. When I went to the hospital to visit the new baby in the nursery, I was unable to keep from crying with joy.

"Crystal is now almost four, and we have a very special relationship that transcends the affection normally shared with honorary visiting aunts. Needless to say, she holds a special place in my heart. She, like Toby, is a joyful child who has brought much happiness to her family."   *L. O. C.*

The story of Linda and Toby offers the happy assurance that the separation caused by death is not permanent. Our deceased loved ones can contact us from the other side of life; and, perhaps even more encouraging, they can return and rejoin us on this side. This is part of the hope that can be found in the concept of reincarnation.

Reincarnation has an important place in the Edgar Cayce material. Understanding re-birth can make it easier to adopt a helpful perspective on death. It can enable us to view two features as a natural part of the soul's journey: death and the return for additional lifetimes. To see how this journey started and where it will lead, let's look back to our beginning.

OUR CREATION

According to Edgar Cayce, all souls were created by God in the very beginning, long before the earth came into being. The reason behind our Father's gift of life to us was "God's desire for companionship and expression . . ." (5749-14) Many of the Cayce readings emphasize that the divine plan is for each of us to become a companion and co-creator with God.

God is love, and so co-creating with Him involves expressing His love for others, which can best be accomplished through attunement to our Creator and service to our fellow beings. This principle is most beautifully summarized in Cayce's words to one person who sought practical advice for living:

Live each and every day as if the evening was to be spent with *thy* Creator, and in the *morning* of each day give thanks to the Creator for that [which you] may be able to give in service and self to others, that they may be blessed ... for he that would be the greatest among men will be the servant of men. Learn what that means in the life, and the life will be worthwhile.   4185-3

So that we might become creative companions with Him, in the beginning God gave each soul free will. We can use this gift to live according to our Father's plan, by manifesting His love. But we also have the freedom to disregard His will and live selfishly. When we choose to live selfishly, we separate ourselves from our Creator. This choice makes it necessary for us to correct our ways—to learn how to live lovingly, in accord with His plan. The basic purpose of our existence on earth is to give us the opportunity to assimilate that lesson. By doing so, we will achieve the ultimate goal of our existence: to regain the loving oneness we had with our Father in the beginning.

REINCARNATION

The achievement of complete reunion with God is likely to take a great deal of time and experience. Most of us are incapable of accomplishing this grand purpose within a single, physical lifetime. To bring that final goal within the reach of every soul, God has given us the additional gift of reincarnation. This provides each of us with as many lifetimes as we need to learn to live in accordance with His loving will.

The basic principles of reincarnation are uncomplicated: the soul is immortal and continues to exist after the death of the body. At various intervals, it can choose to enter a new physical body, in order to gain further experience from an additional lifetime on earth. In some belief systems, reincarnation is thought to include animal lifetimes as well as human ones. According to the Cayce readings, this is *not* how it works. Animals do reincarnate, progressing from one species to another. But the human soul always incarnates into the human family. It may at times, however, choose to change sex from one lifetime to the next.

One of Edgar Cayce's dreams, which he had long after his mother's death, illustrates some of the basic points about reincarnation. In the dream, Mrs. Cayce informed her son that she had been told she would be reborn in nine months to people near and dear to him. According to a subsequent reading, this message about the soul's prospective return for another lifetime was literally true. Since the return and some of its circumstances were foreknown, this incident suggests that rebirth is not a random, accidental event.

This dream also shows us another implication of reincarnation. The soul continues to exist *between* lifetimes on earth. It has consciousness and has experiences that potentially can be remembered later. The preexistence of the soul is an ancient idea—but can it be accepted as fact? While he was on this earth, my husband Bill would have told you that it can.

A SOUL'S EXPERIENCES BEFORE BIRTH

On several occasions I heard Bill tell of his experiences leading up to birth. While still on the other side, he saw many events that were to happen in the latter part of his life, if he were to be born. He witnessed natural disasters, humanity's cruelty toward its fellow human beings, wars, violence, and other visions, which he said were too horrible to mention. Because of what he saw, Bill did not want to come into another physical lifetime! (We have met others who have had this same prebirth experience.)

On the night of his birth into this life, Bill's consciousness was in the upstairs bedroom of the family home. He saw his mother-to-be in bed, very big with child. His father was standing at the foot of the bed. It was a cool night in early October. The street in front of the house was not paved, but was packed hard.

At about 1:30 a.m., Bill heard hoofbeats on the dry street. He then saw a horse-drawn buggy pull up and stop at the brick walk leading to the front porch. The doctor got out, took a hitching block out of the buggy, and snapped the line fastened to it onto the horse's bit. He then took a small black bag out of the buggy and walked up to the house.

My husband's memory, or prebirth awareness, was interrupted at this point. His next recollection was of Christmas time, when he was about three months old. Many years afterward he described this Christmas scene, in minute detail, to his mother. She confirmed the accuracy of his account and said that it reminded her of details she had long since forgotten. During his lifetime my husband saw so many of his prebirth visions come to pass, that it would not have been possible for him to doubt the soul's pre-existence.

But does the soul *always* come into physical life by choice? Edgar Cayce indicated that there may be exceptions. In a reading given for my husband, Mr. Cayce said that Bill had entered only "partly by choice." Having foreseen what was in store for him, my husband had to be "pushed," by the Divine that is within all of us, to enter and face this experience.

The basic purpose of reincarnation is to give us the experiences necessary to teach us to live according to God's plan. For these experiences to help us move toward our goal, we must be able to learn from them. So remembrance of our past lives *could* be quite useful in our spiritual development. Such memories are normally beyond the reach of most of us. But the Cayce readings assure us that we have the ability ultimately to recall everything that ever happened to us, from the moment of creation. This question-and-answer exchange—from Cayce's interpretation of the Book of Revelation—reminds us of Christ's promise to open our memories.

> . . . Let's illustrate by what has been given: The Master gave, "Before the world was, I AM! Now if ye abide in me and I in the Father, then I will bring to thy remembrance ALL *THINGS*—from the foundations of the world!   281-33

Mr. Cayce went on to explain that our consciousness is "dead" to our past lives until we awaken to the Divine within, which then brings to our remembrance all things from the very beginning. Three steps are necessary to awaken this awareness: daily prayer and meditation, service to others, and reading the Bible. They activate our physical, mental, and spiritual natures. Edgar Cayce himself set an excellent example in each of these three practices. So it is not at all surprising that he was able to recall many incidents from his earlier lifetimes.

SODOM AND GOMORRAH REVISITED

Mr. Cayce sometimes had remarkable inner experiences—like visionary dreams—while simultaneously giving a reading. On one occasion, while in the trance state delivering a reading, he relived the part he had played during the destruction of Sodom and Gomorrah. After awakening at the end of the reading, he described his experience, saying that he had seemed to be accompanying Lot and his family as they were fleeing the destruction of the two cities. He spoke of passing through great heat, as of fire from heaven.

The Bible tells us that Sodom and Gomorrah were destroyed because of the liberal practice of sodomy. Scripture relates that two beings appeared and warned Lot, a godly man, that he and his wife should flee because the cities were about to be consumed by fire and brimstone. They were also warned not to turn around and look back once they had left. Lot's wife disobeyed these instructions and was instantly turned into a pillar of salt.

In a later reading, given to explain his experience of this Biblical incident, Cayce was told that he had been one of the messengers sent to make Lot aware of the approaching danger. The purpose of this past-life recall was to warn Cayce of upcoming trials by fire. Not long thereafter he was arrested and jailed for fortunetelling. Having been forewarned, he had an opportunity to prepare for this test.

CHOICE AND KARMA

At its creation each soul was endowed with free will. This attribute gives us repeated opportunities to grow spiritually. With each decision we face, we can move toward life—toward God—or we can take off in the opposite direction. When faced with any choice, it's helpful to have a standard upon which we can base our decision. Many of the Cayce readings stress the importance of carefully establishing an *ideal* toward which we want to work. A thoughtfully selected ideal can help clarify for us what we truly believe in, and it can guide us in making the choices that will allow us to live creatively and lovingly.

Our decisions are so very important because they determine what we make of our lives and ourselves. A beautiful simile is found in the Cayce files: In each seed lies its potential—for example, to become a tree that bears fruit. Each soul, too, may become as a tree of life to many people, nourishing and protecting them. But just as surely, the soul, like a tree, may wither and die. In order to flourish, the soul itself must receive proper nourishment, which it obtains through bringing shelter and sustenance to others. Each soul must eventually become like a corpuscle or cell in the life flow and body of God!

Life is of God. He is the Creator of all that is. Human beings can do things to alter the character of life, but it cannot be ended or destroyed. The destiny of each soul is to return to its Source. How *long* does it take to prepare the soul for its Maker? This depends entirely upon what the soul does with its knowledge of God and with its understanding of the Father's wishes.

Every day there are choices to be made, for good or for evil. These options appear in what we think, what we say, and even what we eat and drink. The choice is ours, and through it we daily create our own destiny. As we go about making our decisions in day-to-day life, we would do well to remember that each of our choices has an effect. Decisions that are in accord with God's will have positive results. Mistakes bring experiences that teach us we have lessons to learn. This is the essence of *karma*, the spiritual law by which we reap what we have sown.

We often experience the results of our mistakes as difficulties. When this happens, we should remember that God is not punishing us for our errors; rather, we are being given an opportunity to learn and to develop by surmounting our problems. It is possible for us to use constructively any condition we meet in life, no matter how difficult we may find it to be.

The law of karma is active throughout our lives. It affects the situation into which we are born and the conditions we meet each day. The law of karma can also influence the time and manner of our passing. Realizing this can help us grasp the meaning behind the death of a loved one. As the following story illustrates, the separation can be particularly hard to accept in cases when someone close to us has met an unexpected end. Yet, hope can be found in knowing that there is a *reason* for such a death, a *necessary lesson* for the soul to learn. Hope comes, too, with the potential of reincarnation, with the possibility that the separation need not be final.

A DECEASED DAUGHTER EXPLAINS HER DEATH

While Bill and I were visiting Spain during 1985, a grieving mother talked with us about her daughter's death. During our conversation, I found it most heartening to see the woman's spirits improve as she began to consider some of the possibilities reincarnation offers.

The story we listened to was about a beautiful thirteen-year-old girl who had fallen to her death while mountain climbing with a friend. For some reason, the girl's mother felt that her daughter had been pushed by her companion, who the mother thought was motivated by jealousy.

Shortly after her death, the daughter appeared to her mother in a dream and explained how she had slipped and fallen. Though she had desperately tried to grasp a bush or the branch of a tree as she fell, she was unable to hang on and plummeted to her death.

I feel that the girl returned and described the unintentional nature of her demise because she realized that her mother thought foul play was involved. By reassuring the woman that this was not the case, the daughter could help her avoid bitterness and perhaps lessen the intensity of her grief.

Though this death was unintended, the Cayce readings tell us that so-called "accidents" never occur without a cause. In this case, a karmic debt or a lesson to be learned by the souls involved must have been at work. For some reason, this was a necessary experience for the girl and her mother.

I explained to the woman that because her daughter was so young when she died, it was quite possible that she could reincarnate quickly, perhaps within a year or two. The mother, who was in her mid-thirties, was filled with joy at this prospect. If she desired to have another child, that child just might be the daughter whom she cared for so much. It is my firm belief that the love of these two souls for each other will make this possible.

THE ROLE OF PHYSICAL DEATH

According to the Cayce material, the purpose of life is to teach us to manifest God's love for others. All our experiences can be used to learn this essential lesson. Death, too, furnishes us with experiences that we can use in our spiritual development. Thus, physical life and death are not opposites. They are but two aspects of a continuing process of spiritual growth. Each plays a part in enabling us to rediscover our relationship with God and achieve our eventual reunion with Him.

Death allows us to experience a different part of our relationship with God than we are able to see during physical life. Death is a step in the soul's journey back to its Creator. From a spiritual point of view, our fear of death is inappropriate. Cayce beautifully described this more enlightened view of death with these words:

The death is separation, and thus man hath dreaded same; yet when it has lain aside its phase that maketh afraid, it is but the birth into *opportunities* that—if they are embraced with Him, the *truth—as* thy guide—will bring joy and harmony into thy experience! 1776-1

At death the conscious mind is laid aside and the subconscious becomes more active. Death is, therefore, a change in consciousness. Through this change we can gain a fresh perspective of the continuing life of the soul. In this way, a dream about death can very likely be a hopeful symbol, rather than a frightening one. The awakening of something new—especially new thoughts or a deeper awareness of our subconscious life—can readily be depicted in our dreams as some sort of death. As Cayce put it to one person who was very worried about a dream in which she died: "This, then, is the awakening of the subconscious, as is manifested in death in physical forces, being the birth in the mental."

(136-6)

The lessons death teaches are valuable to us because of the immortality of the soul. When the physical body passes away, the soul survives and is able to move on to a different type of learning. In future incarnations, it can return into new circumstances and undergo fresh experiences, thus giving a broader understanding of physical life. Each expansion of consciousness brings us closer to comprehending the "infinite influence" of God and our relationship to it. Cayce's advice to one man is good counsel to us all:

. . . it isn't all of life to live, in one experience. For, life is continued; life itself is a consciousness, a gift of an infinite influence we may call God. 2399-1

For the soul to reach an understanding of its relationship with God, it will most likely need a variety of experiences in physical life. This makes death a necessary means of transition from one lifetime to the next. It allows the soul to gain experience in one set of material conditions, exit the physical world, and later come back into another setting.

We can see how well this system works if we think about the cases in which a soul has entered into some limiting situation—such as a severe physical handicap—that is likely to last an entire lifetime. There is always a reason for an individual to incarnate into such circumstances. Perhaps the purpose is to give the soul itself a needed lesson. Or perhaps, as is suggested in our next story, the soul takes on a condition in order to help the people nearby grow in understanding.

Whatever the underlying cause in any specific case, there is a constructive purpose for these experiences. Realizing this can be a source of strength to those touched by long-term disabilities, either their own or others'. And we can be greatly encouraged by the knowledge that even limitations that will probably last until death are not permanent. As the following report compellingly shows, there is always the possibility of greatly expanded opportunities in the future.

A LITTLE CHILD SHALL LEAD THEM

With this account, our narrator gives us a clear picture of the hope we can find if we are able to extend our vision beyond the limits of a single physical lifetime.

"It started quite simply but grew more complex and beautiful as our conversation continued. I was seated at our dining-room table, spoon-feeding a pureed meal to my crippled stepdaughter. My seven-year-old granddaughter sat opposite us, chewing a homemade fruit bar.

My granddaughter and I had just returned from swimming and air-mattress rafting on the nearby Bear River. We were now alone, and the setting was ideal for a good, relaxing rest.

" 'Grandpa,' the young child asked, 'why can't she talk, and why hasn't she any teeth, and why is her back so curved?'

"Let's be careful on this one, I thought, and then responded, 'Perhaps it's just to show you how fortunate you are to have a good, strong body in which to live while you are on this earth, and to teach you to say "Thank You, God" and mean it.'

"I then attempted to explain simply how my step-daughter had received brain damage shortly after birth. Skilled surgeons had been unsuccessful in their effort to remove a foreign growth that had caused the damage. The doctors had said then that she wouldn't live more than three or four years. Today, she is twenty-eight years old and still smiling.

"Next I tried to tell how we have attempted to learn to talk with her through feelings, not words. 'So you see,' I continued, 'she has helped both her mother and me in learning more about our true inner selves, that part of us we call the soul.'

"My stepdaughter reached for my face with her better hand and tugged at my beard. 'She sure does like to pull your beard, doesn't she?' the younger girl observed.

" 'That's how she has learned to express love. You see her toothless smile and the glow in her eyes? That's the main reason I wear a beard,' I explained.

"Don't get too rough on your old grandpa, I thought; yet I was thrilled at the nearness of our inner attunement and released myself for what might come next.

" 'Will she come back next time as a cripple?' Not for one second did I question the authority of such an inquiry from this adjusting young mind. I realized she had not been taught, even simply, about the ins and outs of reincarnation, and so I rightly concluded that her words were not from rote. Her question needed an answer, not a discussion, for she had posed it clearly.

" 'No,' was my definite response.

" 'How do you know?' I very frankly related an experience I had had many years before, one that I've shared with but few; for not many are as ready as this child was proving to be.

" 'Because God has been good to me. He gave me a vision in which I was able to see her in the future.'

" 'What's a vision, Grandpa?'

" 'A vision,' I explained, 'is like a dream, only a person isn't always asleep when it happens, just very quiet. One time long ago I said a prayer, which is simply talking to God. Then I sat really quiet for a little while, not letting myself think of anything, just waiting—waiting to possibly hear from God. This way of thinking— or rather, of not thinking—is called meditation.

" 'While I was being empty of everything in my mind this way, my vision came to me. It was a clear mental picture of a beautiful young woman, whole and hearty, standing on a pedestal among crowds of people. Single people and groups came up to this young woman and seemed to be asking her which way to go. She would look down at them, smile, and point out a direction. The people would then leave, following the directions she had given them.

" 'This picture gradually faded from my mind,' I continued, 'and I was left with a feeling of wonderment. Then a rather startling inspiration came over me as my thoughts went back to her. That's when I knew the woman in my vision had been my stepdaughter. I felt sure that in this way God was giving me encouragement to keep on going. That vision is as clear in my memory today as it was the day I received it. Do you understand now how I know that she will not come back again as a cripple?' I asked.

" 'Yes,' said my granddaughter. And I was sure she truly did understand. Oh, that more of us might assume the simple unadulterated faith of a yet unspoiled child of seven. During this entire conversation, my stepdaughter had sat quietly. I know she gained inwardly, even as did we two who enjoy more nearly perfect physical bodies. My prayer in response was simple: 'Thank You, Father!' ''   *J. S.*

3

SENSING THE APPROACH OF DEATH

ONE OF THE most curious findings of parapsychology is the validity of precognition—the capacity to be aware of seemingly unpredictable events well before they occur. This talent has been substantiated in laboratory research as an authentic human potential. Although only very few individuals can demonstrate precognition on demand, most everyone has had a few experiences in which a dream or hunch came true.

Perhaps the most dramatic displays involve premonitions of death. Of course, some skeptics still wonder if it is really possible for us to have intuitive knowledge of coming events—even those involving death. But the persuasive evidence provided by this story makes it hard to doubt.

"I have been involved with several dreams in which contact was apparently made with people who had died. One that occurred some time in 1973 was presented to me as a challenge by a co-worker at the Aberdeen Proving Ground, in Maryland. This gentleman saw colors whenever he listened to classical music; yet he was unaware that this is a most unusual phenomenon, and he had no knowledge of dream interpretation or any other branch of parapsychology. The challenge he gave me was to find the message in a strange dream he had had.

"In my friend's dream, he met his deceased father and a neighbor named Ike. Ike was teaching my friend's dad how to carve wood. It seemed my friend got a big kick out of this because his dad, who had been a CPA and a musician, had possessed no mechanical aptitude whatsoever and certainly had not been interested in any talent like wood carving.

"Briefly, I told my co-worker that the dream indicated Ike would soon be joining his father. I said that the wood-carving practice could mean his dad was going through a learning phase of some kind. Possibly he was learning patience, a step in spiritual growth. When I gave my friend this interpretation of his dream, he just laughed and said that I was being ridiculous and that he didn't believe a word of what I had told him.

"Two weeks later Ike was dead, apparently of a heart attack." *W. J. W.*

This interesting story reveals several points related to what happens after death. It shows that those who have departed continue to exist, and also that they continue to learn. There are lessons to be assimilated on the other side, just as there are in physical life.

But the most striking feature of this dream is the accuracy of its prediction. The death of a neighbor was foreseen, even though, from the material viewpoint, there had apparently been no indications that the transition was about to occur. This suggests some interesting questions: How can such precise foreknowledge be possible? And how can sensitive individuals foresee coming events?

COMING EVENTS CAST THEIR SHADOWS

In one of his dream experiences, Edgar Cayce found himself on a train with a group of deceased evangelists. They were going to a meeting where the disciple John was to teach. One of the evangelists told the dreamer that he, Cayce, wasn't like the other people there, and so he couldn't go as far on the train as they would. Throughout the trip the people in the group were having a discussion about human nature and how the material universe has its source in the spiritual plane.

With this last point, Mr. Cayce's dream discloses a key principle behind psychic foreknowledge of any kind. Quite a few of the readings convey the same message—that everything which occurs in our world is the result of causes that have been set up in nonmaterial realms: ''. . . all that materializes must first happen in spirit, and the law of cause and effect ever remains.'' (3412-2) These nonmaterial causes must exist before their effects can manifest in the physical. We can experience them as we would shadows cast by coming events.

Psychics and other sensitive people who are able to attune to the nonmaterial planes can see these shadows before the events happen in the physical world. In some cases, the "thought forms" of approaching occurrences are read as "signs" in the heavens. Edgar Cayce often saw clairvoyantly such indicators of the future. Another possibility, illustrated by Cayce's advance knowledge of his mother's death, is for the signs to be sensed while an individual is in a trance state.

Perhaps the shadows of coming events are most commonly encountered in dreams. The Cayce readings tell us that important occurrences in our lives are previewed in this way before they happen: ''. . . for dreams are that of which the subconscious is made, for any conditions ever becoming reality [are] first dreamed.''   (136-7)

The annals of psychical research, like the Bible itself, are full of accounts of accurate foresight received through all these means. For example, many people in Europe dreamed of German soldiers invading their homes before it occurred. Abraham Lincoln was forewarned of his own death in a dream. Similarly, several of my correspondents have received foreknowledge of the approaching death of someone close to them.

EDGAR CAYCE IS WARNED

As might be expected, Edgar Cayce was among the many who have had dreams related to future events. But sometimes the dream provides a warning about something that is likely to happen but still subject to change. This story tells of a case in which he foresaw something that did not occur.

In his dream, Edgar Cayce was a child again, and he saw fairies and elves, as he had in his younger years. He also recognized current friends who during his childhood had been in the spirit world, not yet having been born into physical life.

Since this dream was so unusual, Cayce gave himself a reading to get some insight on its meaning. It was interpreted as a warning that he needed to receive increased encouragement from the people around him to busy himself more deeply in his work. Otherwise, he would soon be drawn into the spirit world—in other words, he would die.

This dream illustrates something that should never be forgotten when we consider intuitive vision into the future: the role of free will in determining what will happen. It is possible for acceptance of psychic foreknowledge to lead us into a type of fatalism. We can erroneously come to believe that our future is definitely set, regardless of what we try to do.

This is not the view of the Edgar Cayce readings. This material consistently emphasizes the importance of the human will: "God Himself knows not what man will destine to do with himself . . . He has given man free will. *Man* destines the body!" (262-86) Thus, what we will experience in life depends upon the decisions we make. Sometimes dreams and other forms of psychic foresight are meant just to show us our possibilities.

Edgar Cayce's dream of being a child again provides a good example of this. If his associates in physical life did not help him appreciate the value of his work here, Cayce might choose to neglect the special gifts God had given him, and this would lead to his death. But he also had the option of continuing to use his talents in the material world. Doing so would enable him to keep on living. The decision was his. (As a matter of fact, Mr. Cayce lived for over thirteen years after having this warning dream.)

In other cases, precognitive information seems to show a future which is highly likely to unfold because of choices already made. Most of the material I have received from my correspondents describing foreknowledge falls into this category. Here the purpose is not to give a warning so that premature death can be avoided. Rather, it is to inform the recipient that the time for a transition is approaching, so that the coming passage can be prepared for. Often this simply involves mental preparation on the part of the people affected. At other times, there is something to be done before a loved one moves on. Our next story gives a vivid example of this type of experience.

A PRECOGNITIVE EXPERIENCE OF DEATH

I received this account from a woman whose intuitive feelings enabled her to re-establish contact with her family while there was still time. We can easily imagine that having made this visit helped her cope with her parent's passing when it did occur.

"In October of 1980 I felt a strong urge to travel to our family home in California for the holidays. I discussed this with my husband, and he said there must be something to it, as I don't usually get these impelling urges unless there is a good reason. So when the time came, we made the trip. This was the first Christmas in over thirty years that the entire family was able to be together; and as it turned out, it was to be the last.

'The following September, my father passed away. We had been warned before his death occurred. During our last visit, my father told me that he had been touched lightly on the back of his head many times in the preceding weeks. I did not wish to alarm him or any of the others, so I merely said, 'Ah ha! Someone is trying to get your attention.'

"At 6:15 on the morning of August 31, 1981, he collapsed in the bathroom of my parents' home. At that moment I, in Jacksonville, Florida, experienced a severe ringing in my right ear. After glancing at the clock, I told my husband, 'Something bad has happened to someone close to me.' My mother's call later in the morning confirmed my premonition."   *D. T.*

An interesting point about this story is that my correspondent's father himself evidently did not recognize the warning touches on his head for what they were. The person who is to make the transition is not always the one to realize consciously what's about to occur. But, as our next report shows, sometimes a soul does indeed know that the time to move on is near.

A PRECOGNITIVE AND TELEPATHIC EXPERIENCE

In this story, our narrator's father expresses after death the same concern for his family that he had before passing on. This is an encouraging feature, for it shows that the more noble and selfless elements of our character do not disappear at death.

*   *   *

"My father had been paralyzed for eighteen months due to a stroke. One morning as I was sleeping, I dreamed that he and I were talking. He was telling me how to treat my mother after he died. Mother was very temperamental and inclined to hysterics.

"Some time later the phone rang, and my husband woke up and left the room to answer it. While he was talking, I was hurriedly dressing. He came back into our bedroom to awaken me and tell me Pop had died. I told him that I already knew! We rushed over to my parents' apartment and found it to be true."   *P. F.*

This ongoing love and concern for family members left behind in the physical world is well illustrated in another story. Here a wife urgently communicates the need for her husband to grow spiritually.

A MOTHER'S VISIT

This report, describing a visit from my correspondent's deceased mother, plainly shows the urgent concern that a soul on the other side can have for the spiritual well-being of a loved one still in the physical.

"In a dream of August 13, 1985, I saw a desk and knew that my deceased mother was nearby, though I did not see her. I said, 'Mama, may I talk to you?'

"She answered in her natural, cheerful voice. Her laughter was real and very happy. She quickly began telling me about my dad and brothers doing some work for a neighbor and the difficulty they were having. Then her voice began to fade. I kept wondering why she was telling me all this instead of listening to what I said. I felt she was rushed for time and I asked, 'Is Dad going to die soon?'

"She responded by asking, 'Does he know?'

"I was perplexed by this, because I thought she

would know everything. I hesitated and said, 'He wouldn't be surprised.'

"Another female voice, with a German accent, cut in sharply and said, 'Your mother is tired and she has to leave.'

"Mom's voice faded in and out as she continued to talk to me. Although I can't recall the entire conversation, at one point I said, 'I am sorry, I can neither hear nor understand you.' After a moment's silence I could hear her voice more clearly.

"Then I asked her what I could do for my dad more than I was already doing. Her answer surprised me as she said, 'You are not doing anything for him! Feeding him is not work. You should minister to his soul.'

"My father is a good man, but he rarely attends church. He says he loves the Lord, but he refuses to be baptized. I asked my mother, 'Should he be baptized?'

"She said, 'Certainly!'

"Then I said, 'May I ask you . . .' But she cut me off, saying, 'You may ask no more.' Later I relayed the message to my father, but he still refuses to be baptized."

L. S.

Our next story concerns another dream in which an approaching death is foreseen. Here we notice the same natural concern for one's family as was shown in the preceding accounts. This incident is a bit unusual in that the connection between the dreamer and the subject of the dream is more distant than is commonly the case.

ANOTHER ACCURATE PREMONITION

One of the features that sets this story apart is our narrator's reluctance to tell anyone about the dream. As we will see from the story, this reaction is quite understandable. But it can cause us to wonder: How many accurate premonitions are received, but never reported?

"When I was ten years old, I dreamed I was walking along the sidewalk in front of a friend's house. Her father approached me and said that he would like me to do a favor for him. In the dream I knew that he was dead, but I did not feel in any way startled or alarmed by him. I asked what favor he wanted, and he replied that he would like me to tell his wife that he was well and happy. I knew that for some reason I was more receptive to his message than his wife was, and that he had been unable to contact her himself. I woke up before I said that I would pass the message on.

"In reality, my friend's father was not dead. She was not really a close friend, and I felt awkward about telling her I had dreamed her father was deceased, so I decided not to. A few weeks later, he had a heart attack and died.

"At that point I was even more hesitant to tell her, because after the fact not only would I probably not be believed, but I also would be intruding on the family's grief. I also feared that I would be accused of inventing the story just to get attention for myself. You see, I was not a very confident child. So I never did tell my friend about the dream. But this incident still seems to me to be a real experience with the other side." *C. B.*

EXTRAORDINARY KNOWLEDGE OF DEATH

The following stories are from people who have received knowledge of another's death through some means beyond ordinary physical communication. In many of these cases—though not all—the source of the information appears to be the departed soul itself. Such incidents can help us realize more clearly our own potential as human beings, for they show that the soul is not bound by the body, and that it continues to exist and to be able to communicate after the body has died.

In most of these accounts it seems that knowledge of the transition was received at or slightly after the moment of death. Thus the majority of these incidents are not examples of foreknowledge, since they involve events that had already happened. Yet, we do have strong evidence for the validity of these experiences, in that through them people received verifiable information that they could not have known by ordinary means.

This is clearly seen in our first report, in which my correspondent was contacted by someone who had met a completely unexpected death. We have here a fascinating combination of terror at the beginning of the incident, followed by complete calmness. Perhaps the message is that one's fear of death can be much worse than the actual passing.

CONTACT WITH A DEPARTED FRIEND

This story is remarkable for the precise correspondence in time between our narrator's experience and the event it signified. It would be hard to come up with a more convincing demonstration that the soul does not perish with the demise of the body.

"I awoke at two o'clock in the morning, lying on my back in a state of total paralysis. I could not even move my eyes to the right or the left, but could see only peripherally. I became terrified, but I was unable to call out to my roommates for help.

"I then noticed, within my peripheral range of vision, a small object floating by the upper left corner of the facing wall. It was a yellow butterfly, with the markings of a monarch; but in the center was the image of a human face. The face resembled my friend T. P., but I did not sense that it was he. At this point my fear was becoming unbearable, bordering on complete panic.

"The butterfly then floated toward me from the upper left, touched me upon the heart, and drifted away to the upper right until it disappeared. At the moment it touched my heart, all my fears and tension melted away. I calmly rolled over, noted the time on my alarm clock, and fell back to sleep until late in the morning.

"I learned later that T. P. had been killed in an automobile accident just prior to my experience. Interestingly, he had once had a premonition of his early demise. This forewarning had led to his being tested at the state university, but no ESP abilities were detected.

"Even now, writing of this experience has a very strong emotional impact on me. In my mind I have come to understand the butterfly as my deceased friend, in distress at his own passing, returning to console me. Several months after the incident, I came across the information that the butterfly motif had been used by ancient Egyptians as a representation of the resurrected soul."
                                                    J. N.

The possibility that fear of the approach of death is worse than death itself can be seen in our following report as well. The frightening part of the experience it describes happened before the actual transition, which in itself was peaceful.

PENETRATING "THE VALLEY OF THE SHADOW OF DEATH"

This account was received from a woman who has contributed a great deal of material to this book. Here, in addition to an interesting story, she offers a reasonable explanation for the contrast between her mother's ominous vision and the tranquility of the death it foretold.

"My adoptive mother has had several experiences with death and souls who have passed on. One of the oddest goes back to the World War II era. Her father had been a semi-invalid, with rheumatoid arthritis, for over twenty years. Then he developed flu, which went into pneumonia. With his crippled back this was, of course, especially serious, because of the problem it caused him with breathing. Therefore, his wife, my mother, and a private nurse took turns sitting with him.

"Mom's shift had just ended, and the nurse thought the elderly man seemed much more comfortable. But when Mom went down to the kitchen to fix a snack, she suddenly found herself inside a pillar of darkness, which no light or sound could penetrate. Somehow she broke free and phoned the doctor, who arrived just in time for her father's passing. In a few moments she heard her dad call the names of numerous dead relatives, and then he peacefully crossed over.

"But what had Mom met in the kitchen? Of deep and abiding Christian faith, neither she nor her father would ever have seen death as 'blackness.' The best explanation is that possibly the cloud represented 'the shadow of death.' "

                                                        C. P. P.

This story raises an intriguing question: Just what was the significance of the names the dying man called out? Could it be that he was sensing departed relatives who were coming to meet him on the other side, as Mrs. Cayce's deceased parents had come to aid her passage?

Our next report describes a direct encounter with a departing soul, perhaps at the very moment of its passing. This precise correspondence in time gives us a strong indication of the experience's validity. It is interesting that at the time, my correspondent knew neither the identity of the soul involved nor the exact reason for its need. But this knowledge was not necessary. The important thing is that the dreamer knew how to respond to the dream.

THE PEARL OF GREAT PRICE

This story has a striking sense of urgency. Whether or not the departing soul itself was aware of what was needed, our narrator most certainly was. Thus, there was an important purpose behind this vision.

"I awakened, sharply, at 1:30 a.m. from a very vivid dream or vision. In the center of my right hand was a small, egg-shaped pearl, clear and almost transparent. As I held it and looked at it in the palm of my hand, I knew it was a lost soul who was in great need of prayer. I said, 'Oh, I must pray very hard, now—RIGHT NOW— or this soul will die.'

"At this point having awakened from the vision, I started praying; then I meditated a little while and prayed again. When I went back to bed, I prayed until I fell asleep. At 5:30 that same morning, I was awakened by a telephone call from my brother, who told me that our dad had crossed over at 1:30 a.m.

"About a year earlier, during a visit one afternoon, my dad and I had talked on the subject of death. I had asked him where he thought he'd go when he died. He had answered, 'Just six feet under, and that's the end.' I remember trying to tell him about our spiritual body living on, but he had not seemed to believe it.

"Was my father the pearl of my dream? I think so! I still pray for him whenever he comes to mind, and I now feel at peace about him."   *B. J. G.*

The following report tells of an explicit message from the soul of someone who had passed on. In light of the preceding account and some of the other material we've seen so far, the content of that message might seem surprising: that the dreamer's prayers were not needed now.

THE POWER OF PRAYER

The contributor of this story introduces us to an appealing acquaintance who pays her a visit from the other side of life. What but her prayers could have prompted him to make this call?

"When I was a teen-ager, I had a Sunday school teacher who believed firmly in the power of prayer. Each of us in the class would select a section of the carpet to serve as our 'prayer rugs,' and she'd tell us some of the wonderful Biblical stories about healing.

"Shortly after this period, my mother happened to mention to me that our gas-station attendant, who had cancer, had moved to Florida to regain his health. I had always liked this man because of his twinkling blue eyes and the smile and cheery hello he had for children. I prayed earnestly every night for about two months that he would recover.

"At the end of the two months, I had a dream about the gas-station attendant. He was standing, still in his overalls, in a bright place. He said 'I'm O.K. now. You can stop praying for me now.'

"About two weeks later I learned that he had passed on in Florida."   *S. B. W.*

At first glance, we might think that the station attendant's death and his message to the dreamer indicate that the prayers offered were ineffective. But a careful reading of the story does not lead to this conclusion. The very fact that the soul visited this particular person suggests that he was aware of the prayers being said for him and recognized how important they were. We can easily believe that the prayers helped bring him to the "bright place" in which he was seen or allowed him to reach it more quickly. Upon close examination, his words ("I'm O.K. now. You can stop praying for me now.") clearly imply that the prayers had been beneficial up to the point where he became "O.K."

Our next story is another that tells of a dreamer who wakes up with the knowledge that an unexpected death has occurred. Once again, the accuracy of this impression indicates that the experience was truly a visit from the deceased. This account gives us a simple, clear picture of the contentment a soul can find in the afterlife, and it shows as well how a specific personality trait— in this case, concern for one's attire—can be carried over to the other side.

A HAPPY SOUL

One of the interesting features of the dream related here is that it doesn't actually say that the man who appeared in it had died; and yet, my correspondent suspected that precognition or telepathy must be at work here.

"Years ago I was friendly with a man named Blakemore, who at seventy years of age was financially poor and wore patched clothing, but always appeared well dressed. One night I dreamed that Blakemore came through the doorway into my room and asked me to look at his clothes. They were magnificent—perfect in every way.

"When I woke up, I realized Blakemore was dead. I knew he finally was able to dress as he wished. I telephoned his partner Maury and asked how things were going. 'Sadly!' he answered. 'Blakemore dropped dead on Wall Street after dinner last night.' " *C. W.B.*

Like the preceding report, our next story shows that the key to a dream's meaning is sometimes found not in its literal content, but in the dreamer's emotional reaction to it. Despite their somber tone, the dreams related below offer the hope that can be found in knowing that personality, affection, and the desire to communicate survive physical death.

LOVE DOES NOT DIE

When faced with death, two of the most encouraging thoughts we can bear in mind are that love does not pass away and that reconciliation is always possible—even from beyond the grave. In this account, our narrator effectively reminds us of both these truths. Like many of the other stories in this chapter, a dream informed her of a loved one's death before the news came to her in waking life.

"My husband and I were divorced in 1955, and later I married someone else but divorced again. Some time after, I wrote my first husband a letter, and he responded.

"In May 1975 while taking my usual Sunday afternoon nap, I had a vivid dream involving this first husband. We were walking down some steps into a ballroom. He was wearing a full-dress Marine Corps uniform, and we began to waltz. The dream ended on this note, and I awoke feeling very sad and depressed. Later on, I learned that he had left the earth plane.

"In 1978 I had another dream, in which he came to me and said, 'Baby, I am so sorry for so many things.'

" 'It's all right,' I replied. 'We both made mistakes.' "   *D. T.*

Our next dream account, which incorporates both graphic detail and intuitive interpretation, is notable for the accuracy of its timing and content. It is representative of hundreds of similar stories that come from war-related deaths.

A HORRIFYING EXPERIENCE

Here our contributor describes two dreams related to her husband's passing. This account gives us a strong sense of the closeness between the couple, which endured even after my correspondent's spouse was killed.

"I married my boyfriend in May 1941. At that time he was a soldier on his last leave.

"Soon after our wedding I had a dream in which the two of us were walking together through clearly visualized terrain. My wedding ring slipped off my finger. I turned to my husband for help, but he was not there! I found only a stick with his hat on it. I told myself that this was a 'Hollywood' dream of the times and that I should forget it.

"On September 13, 1944, I woke up screaming, having seen my husband's death in a dream. My screams woke my mother, and we noted the date. In my dream I saw a very large meat grinder. Two hands were holding my husband and putting him into the grinder feet first. And, horror of horrors, the hands that held my husband were God's!

"As often happens with my dreams, I seemed to receive a kind of running interpretation—an awareness, a knowing of the meaning. In this case, the message was 'Fear not. He is in my hands.' After the dream I was aware of my husband's presence with me in my room at night—a feeling of deep love and a desire to communicate.

"On October 24, 1944, I received notice that my husband had been killed in action September 13 in Italy. In 1946 his army officer came to visit, which I feel is a very bad custom. He went into great detail about the battle, the terrain, and the manner of my husband's death. After describing the land and the action (my mother said her hair stood on end to hear him using the same words and picturing the same place as I had in telling her my dream), he said that my husband had received a direct hit, from tank fire, in his lower body.

"Strange, yes—but true."   R. S.

The event pictured in the second dream is certainly frightening. But along with the fear there is the comforting message that even when a person meets a violent and untimely death, he or she is never beyond the reach of a loving Father.

FORETELLING THE DEATH OF A LOVED ONE

I have received a number of reports showing that souls in the afterlife are aware of the transitions of others. Several of these accounts indicate that those on the other side can have foreknowledge of death approaching people to whom they were close in physical life. Apparently, souls that have moved on to other dimensions are able to see beyond the bounds of time and space. We have already seen several cases in which previously departed souls either were waiting to greet loved ones as they crossed over or promised they would be there when the time came. These incidents show that the deceased are aware of the time when others pass over.

In the two stories that follow, a close relationship has existed between a soul already in the afterlife and the one whose coming transition of which the soul is aware. Perhaps the *need* of the transiting soul is the motivating force—the need to be received by loved ones who have already made the crossing. We might even imagine that the reunion is an important and eagerly awaited event on the other side, just as birth into the physical is here on this side.

The following stories tell of departed souls informing living relatives of the recent or approaching death of a third family member. In each of these cases, there is a strong purpose for this communication. Information of this sort is not given out arbitrarily. In these two cases the purpose was to prepare the living for news of the passing of a loved one. Both these stories indicate that this opportunity to prepare was truly beneficial.

A CASE OF PRECOGNITION

Here again our contributor tells of the deceased giving advance warning of a death in the family. A clearer, less ambiguous statement of the coming event could hardly be asked for.

"I visited a woman in a rest home who was very ill, and afterwards I went to see her daughter. Before I could say anything to the younger woman, she said to me, 'My dead father came to me and told me that my mother would join him very soon.'

"Therefore, the daughter was not so shocked when,

in fact, her mother did pass on unexpectedly a few weeks later.''
S. C.

PREPARATION FROM A
DECEASED GRANDMOTHER

This report concerns a passing that had already taken place when our narrator heard of it. Nevertheless, she obviously found hope and comfort in this demonstration that our deceased loved ones continue to be near to us.

"My grandmother, with whom I was very close, died. One day shortly after her death, as I was walking through the Randolph Street Station of the Illinois Central Railroad, I had one of those strange experiences. The station was jammed with people, but I was unaware of them.

"Suddenly my deceased grandmother was walking with me and talking in the same quiet voice she had used all her life. She told me that Auntie Bess, who had been seriously ill, had just died. When I reached home, I found it to be true. How wonderful to know that there is no death of the soul and that we can communicate— especially in emergencies!"
P. F.

Taken together, the stories in this chapter create a clear conclusion: states of consciousness beyond the familiar boundaries of time and space allow the perception of coming deaths. We might well wonder why such precognitive impressions do not happen more often. Why do so many deaths come as a surprise to those left behind?

Perhaps the answer lies with the pervasive fear of death in our culture and doubts about survival. The Cayce readings suggest that both fear and doubt are blocks to higher perception. As more and more people shed their fears and replace their doubts, we can expect that helpful premonitions of death will become more commonplace.

4

THE TRANSITION

THE IMAGE OF dying as being like a bridge—as a transition from one form of life to another—is the essence of the stories in this chapter. For some people the greatest uncertainty and fear is not so much the afterlife realm itself but instead the *process* of leaving one world for another. Of course, not every soul experiences the transition in a smooth, peaceful way. However, with understanding and preparation, this birth into a new life can be a joyful occasion. Our first story illustrates that ideal.

A HEAVENLY EXPERIENCE

In this account our contributor paints a delightful picture of a joyful passage and the ability of a soul to communicate its happiness from the other side.

"My husband's mother had entered a nursing home in 1978, and towards Valentine's Day of 1979 we noticed that she was beginning to fail. I was glad that some months earlier she and I had discussed the afterlife and its possibilities.

"Even though my mother-in-law was familiar with the Edgar Cayce readings, she had many doubts about her future. During our last conversation on this matter, she said with a twinkle in her eye, 'Well, if what you say is true, I will let you know.'

"On one occasion when I visited her in April, she said, 'There are nice young men who come in late at night and feed us delicious soup and sandwiches.' Based on my experience with the Cayce material, I could assume from this that she was probably getting help in making her transition.

"My mother-in-law crossed over one July day at 5:00 a.m. My husband and I were having a cup of tea the morning of her passing. We discussed happy memories, as people often do at such times. After a few minutes I began to experience overwhelming feelings of joy, such as I had seldom felt before. I wanted to dance and sing.

"I hugged myself and smiled at my husband. He noted the time as 5:25, and together we rejoiced that his mother had passed on. We felt she was letting us know that all was well.

"We went out that day and took care of all the arrangements. We truly did not grieve, but felt renewed—as we knew she did, too."   *D. T.*

Here we have a description of a gentle transition. Though the mother-in-law had viewed her approaching death with some uncertainty, her doubts do not seem to have seriously impaired her passing. Perhaps the help she received from her nighttime visitors gave a needed boost to her faith. The last sentence of her daughter-in-law's account expresses an interesting and important concept: that in death we can experience not an ending, but a renewal.

DEATH AS A NEW BEGINNING

The encouraging principle of death as a renewal can be found in many of the Edgar Cayce readings. Often Cayce used an idea from the epistles of St. Paul that the dying out of the old is actually an essential part of the renewal of life (Rom. 6:4, 5 and I Cor. 15:36, among others). Thus the death of the body is truly not an extinction, but merely a transition into a new state of being.

On another occasion, Cayce reminded someone that "Dying is not blotting out, it is transition . . ." (1158-9) Putting away the old self can bring the opportunity of a new phase of development. The same sense of death as a new beginning is seen in Cayce's answer to the following question:

> Q. What is meant by "The first shall be last and the last shall be first"?

> A. As illustrated, when life ends it begins. The end is the beginning of the transposition, or the change. The first is last, the last is first. Transposition.   262-39

THE EMPTY URN

In this brief account, my correspondent shares with us an interesting and humorous dream, but one with a very important point: The death of the body is not the end of existence.

"After my father's death I had many experiences of contact with him. But before these experiences began, I had the following dream: I was standing at the family gravesite, where my father's urn, supposedly containing his ashes, was placed. In the dream the metal urn was empty except for a note that read, 'Father is not here any more.' "

                              G. V. P. F.

Here we can see that the dead are no longer confined to the physical. The true self does not die and turn to ashes. With the death of the body it merely takes on a new form—one that cannot be contained within an urn—and moves on to another state of being. One Cayce reading gives a straightforward assurance of the survival of death and tells us what kind of change awaits us: ''For there is no death when the *entity* or the real self is considered; only the change in the consciousness of being able to make application in the sphere of activity in which the entity finds self.'' (2147-1) The transition is a necessary change in consciousness. At death we take on a different type of awareness, one that is suitable to our new environment and will enable us to function in it.

PREPARATION AND HELP IN THE TRANSITION

Several of the reports I have received carry an interesting suggestion about the transition at death. They imply that the change need not be made all at once. At least some individuals are given a chance to prepare themselves, to get their feet wet before diving into their new state of being. Like Edgar Cayce's mother, they are able to make a temporary visit to the other side before their final passage.

Our next account, which actually describes two separate incidents, includes the story of a woman who made such a visit right before her death. The earlier experience, which is related second in this report, shows once again the concern a departed soul can have for family members left behind. In both cases an interesting and rather unusual method is used to get the message across.

A HEAVENLY PERFUME

This report was sent to me by a woman who had faced a very difficult decision near the time of her aunt's transition—whether or not to give the doctors permission to disconnect the life-support systems. The aunt's pre-death visit to the other side gave our narrator some unexpected and extremely welcome input.

"In 1983 my aunt began having small strokes. Having use of her car upon our arrival in California on the previous day, my mother and I had stopped at a supermarket to purchase some supplies. We had closed and locked the car, as it was raining.

"When we returned to the car, I put my mother in the passenger side and got behind the wheel. Mother said, 'What a lovely perfume you are wearing.'

"I said, 'It's not mine. I didn't put any on this morning. It must be yours.'

"'It's not mine, either,' she replied.

"The essence was heavenly. Immediately I thought of my aunt and said, 'Hey, she is over there on the other side, and she's letting us know that all is well.'

"I was especially elated at this evidence since I had to make the final decision with her doctor to disconnect the life-support systems and let her go. This message that she sent told me that she was ready and the right choice was evident. A few days later my aunt passed on.

"A year earlier, in July of 1982, I had had a similar experience with the sense of smell. This incident involved my deceased father, who made his transition after he had moved my mother from California to Florida. As my mother and I were driving past a house that he had once shown interest in buying, an odor became very noticeable in the car—the odor of the intensive care unit that he had been in at the time of his transition. I said aloud, 'Don't worry about Mom, Pops. We'll take good care of her.'"

D. T.

In our next story we can see a different type of preparation for death. Here it is not indicated that the woman actually visited the other side before her passing. But she evidently was able to see and communicate with beings in the spirit realm while she was still in the physical. Like Edgar Cayce's mother and the woman who received soup and sandwiches prior to her crossing, this person received aid before her transition—and from some very special sources.

SPECIAL HELP FOR A DEAR LADY

In this account my correspondent has given us another clear description of a joyous and peaceful death. We can also see how very real the visions were to the woman who was about to make the transition.

"I knew a dear, sweet soul—a college teacher—who gave much of her life in loving service to others. One day when she was well into her eighties and on her deathbed, her niece walked into her bedroom. The younger woman was perplexed to see her aunt with her right arm outstretched and a lovely smile on her face.

"When asked what she was doing, the aunt looked up and said, 'Why, don't you see Him? It's Jesus. He's helping me.'

"On the day of the woman's transition, her niece walked in just as she was about to get out of bed. The niece naturally asked where she was going.

"In surprise, the older woman answered, 'Can't you see him? It's Edgar Cayce. He's telling me to "get up and let's go to work." '

"Soon she was gone."   *E. W.*

Our next account conveys the same heartening message that help is available to souls as they make the transition. Here we can also see that the assistance continues on after death. Like the previous story, this report shows that there are things to be done after death. Even a departed soul's concern for the living should not be allowed to hinder its progress along the path of spiritual development. This need for continued growth on the other side is one of the items that makes the service performed by "greeters" in the spirit realm so valuable.

A LOVING GRANDMOTHER—A GREETER

The narrator of this account has given us a very appealing portrait of a greeter in the next world. Notice that these special souls do not necessarily have to be relatives of the deceased; the quality of love they give forth is far more important than physical kinship.

"One night as I lay in bed I experienced what I consider to have been a contact with the other side. I don't believe I was dreaming since what happened was different from any of my previous dreams. And I had never experienced anything like this during meditation.

"My recently deceased uncle's presence appeared to me, along with that of my grandmother, who had died about two years before. (This uncle and grandmother were not related, but they knew each other very well.) I did not actually see their bodies or faces, but I felt their presence and I knew who they were. I was also aware of a cool mist and a dim yellow haze in the distance.

"I sensed my uncle's anger and knew that he was concerned about the well-being of my aunt, who was still in physical life. He was anxious about her ability to cope with his death and the loneliness she would experience. I told him that she was just beginning to realize he was gone and that she was having difficulty accepting his death. However, I reassured him that my family was doing everything possible to help her and would continue to see that she was taken care of. I also told him that it was now O.K. for him to 'let go' and follow my grandmother.

"I could feel my grandmother's smile and her warmth. Love radiated from her. I don't remember words being spoken by her, but her thoughts were transmitted to me without speech. She explained that her purpose on the other side was to meet those souls recently departed from the earth and help them with their transition. She was very happy and considered it a great honor to be allowed to do this, and I was very happy for her.

"I felt my uncle's relief and knew that he, too, would now be all right. I have not been aware of his presence since that time."   *V. L. R.*

THE EXPERIENCE OF DEATH

In recent years there have been an increasing number of reports of near-death experiences, in which the soul evidently leaves the body and makes a temporary visit to the other side. Several of my correspondents have undergone experiences of this sort. Most of their reports will be presented in Chapter 11 of this book, but it seems appropriate to consider one here as part of our examination of how a soul makes the transition.

Descriptions of these journeys into the next world are intriguing since they may furnish some idea of what death holds in store for us. If so, we have good reason to take heart. For though the accounts I've gathered show some differences in various details, the majority of them give the impression that the soul has been to "a good place"—to use the words of our next story.

A NEAR-DEATH EXPERIENCE

This report gives us several revealing details of the death process. It's particularly interesting that our contributor's mother knew intuitively that it was not yet her time to die and that evidently she felt no fear during the experience itself—only afterward.

"This experience happened to my mother while she was giving birth to my older brother. After the medical staff had given her ether, my mother felt herself rising above the room. She turned and saw herself on the table, with all the nurses around her. Then she sensed that she was being pulled through a tunnel 'backwards.'

"After a time, my mother saw quite a large group of people in front of her, all dressed in white. They asked her how she felt. It seemed that they all spoke at once, like a chorus. My mother replied that it felt as though where they were would be a good place to go when you're ready, but she knew she wasn't ready yet.

"The group then told her that she could go back. 'But,' they said, 'you will never forget what it feels like to be dead.'

"The nurses later told my mother that she had taken a 'nice little nap' and that all her vital signs had been normal throughout. According to my mother, for the next several weeks the experience kept 'coming back' to her, as though she could feel it almost happening again. This frightened her for a good many years, until I started researching near-death experiences. But she now knows that the soul survives bodily death."

R. J. G.

Reports like this one, which tell of people who seemingly make part of the transition we know of as death and then return to physical life, indicate that death is not necessarily an instantaneous event. The Cayce readings often point to the same conclusion. The emerging awareness of having died can occur over a certain period of time, depending on the person's beliefs and the way in which the body's demise comes about. When Cayce was asked in one reading about this, he made a surprising response: "As to how long—many an individual has remained in that [which is] called death for what ye call *years* without realizing it was dead!" (1472-2)

We might find it surprising—perhaps even shocking— to think that a person could be dead for years and not even know it! But consider what might happen at the demise of a person who is thoroughly convinced that physical death is the absolute end of existence. In such an individual's view, there would be no possibility of continued consciousness once the body had met its end. So the very fact that the soul survived and was still aware could well be taken as "proof" that death had not yet occurred.

The confusion may be partly caused by a certain similarity in consciousness before and after the transition. We can see this similarity in many accounts of neardeath experiences, which show that during these journeys the soul still has a sense of physical location and orientation. These reports are consistent with the Cayce readings, which tell us that at death the soul does not leap immediately from the physical to the completely nonmaterial. It is still connected to matter and aware of it—just in a somewhat different form.

After making the transition, the soul is in some ways like a baby newly born into the earth. Just as a newborn needs time to become able to sense and to be aware of its physical surroundings, a recently departed soul often takes time to grow in its awareness of its new environment. And just as different people advance at different rates in this world, in the next there are also variations in the pace of individual development.

A gradual development of consciousness is most often the way a soul experiences the transition, slowly gaining awareness of being in a spirit world. But it is possible for a soul to retain fully its awareness throughout the transition and to recognize its condition. As an example, Cayce was once asked what Jesus had meant by "paradise" in speaking to the thief on the cross. In the reading he replied that Jesus was referring to ". . . the awareness of being in that state of transition between the material and the spiritual phases of consciousness of the soul." (262-92) This answer assures us that the death of the body does not mean extinction, but merely a change from the material state to the spiritual. In simple language, Jesus was saying to the thief, "There is no death."

The material I have collected constantly assures us that death is not the end of life. The continuity of existence is illustrated in each of the two brief stories that follow. Although the first account does not deal with the transition of any particular soul, nevertheless it illustrates an important point: something deep within the mind of the soul knows about the continuity of life and tries to remind us of this fact, even through dream messages.

THE MUMMY AWAKENS

In this account, our narrator relates a dream in which the key element is a very appropriate symbol for the preservation of life.

"One night I dreamed that I had dug up a mummy in my potato patch. The mummy got up from its sarcophagus, unwound its wrappings, and ran happily off.

"A strange dream, but rather nice. Weeks later I understood what it meant: There is no death."   *B. J. N.*

A MESSAGE FROM A DECEASED FATHER

This story gives us a simple, straightforward statement of the continuity of life. The daughter's reaction to this message clearly shows the impact of recognizing the reality of survival.

"I know of a young girl who believed in survival after physical death. She dreamed that she had returned to her father's funeral. When she arrived, he was lying on his bed. He looked up at her and smiled. She screamed and shouted, 'You're alive! You're alive!'

"Her father spoke, saying, 'It's all right. You understand now that I am not dead.' Then she heard him say, 'Give them flowers while they are alive.' "   *G. D.*

It's interesting that Edgar Cayce, too, advised sending flowers to the living. The dead are unconscious and therefore cannot appreciate them; or, if "awake" in the afterlife they will be moving on and cannot take the flowers along. A lady whom Mr. Cayce had known well often made this same point. This friend, a flower retailer who made many sales to Cayce, emphasized that sending the plants to the dead meant nothing, since they could be neither smelled nor enjoyed. She suggested that they be given to the living—the ill, the old, the lonely—who could value their beauty, their fragrance, and the thoughts and prayers that usually accompanied them.

Edgar Cayce dreamed of this woman at the very time that she was being buried in a local cemetery. Since she had strongly believed that death was actually a birth into another life, her appearance in the dream fittingly symbolized the survival of the soul. This message was repeated in another dream, which Mr. Cayce had on the same night as the one about the florist friend:

A VISIT FROM THREE DECEASED FRIENDS

Edgar Cayce's dream that night—which was shortly after the end of World War I—included a graveyard scene. I once heard Cayce state about graveyards, "I can honestly say that there are very few cemeteries that do not appear familiar to me. If I just see a corner of a cemetery, I can immediately tell a good deal about it." In this particular dream he was in France, viewing the burial sites of many soldiers. Among the graves were those of three boys who had been in his Sunday school class.

Suddenly, to Cayce's surprise, the three young men appeared alive before him! They looked the same as they had on the day they had bidden him good-bye while in their earthly bodies. Each described the circumstances of his death. One had been killed by machine-gun fire, another when he had been caught in the midst of a shell burst, and the third in a heavy artillery barrage. Toward the end of the scene, two of the boys gave Cayce messages to relay to their loved ones at home.

A reading obtained to interpret this dream said that it represented the continuation of the material world after death. This is seen most clearly in the boys' eagerness to send messages to those they had left behind in the physical plane, and it is also shown by their unchanged appearances and their unimpaired memory of their deaths.

So far we have looked at quite a few dreams that illustrate the unity between the material and the spiritual phases of our existence. But we should not think that we have to sleep and dream to be shown that life continues beyond the grave. Our next two stories describe *waking contact* with recently departed souls. In both of them we can see the soul's desire to communicate with the living and its ability to influence the material plane.

A POLTERGEIST EXPERIENCE

As this story shows, the dead not only continue to exist, they are really not so far removed from our own world as we might think. It is also possible to detect here an amusing combination of affection and vexation on the part of my correspondent.

"This incident was in the nature of a poltergeist experience. Three days after my grandfather's death, I felt his presence, and the lights in my apartment began to flicker. I checked the bulbs and found that they were tight and nothing else was wrong. When I entered the bedroom, the same thing happened to the lights there. The next time it was the hall lights that went on and off in a rhythmic manner. This occurred for about half an hour each night.

"Annoyed, I asked my grandfather to please stop! The third night I dreamed he was doing this to attract my attention. To emphasize this, in my dream he threw a wicker chair at me to say hello!"   *S. R.*

The following report tells of communication between the living and the dead that apparently required a certain amount of effort from both participants. Perhaps both parties were motivated by the same desire to say good-bye.

AN EDUCATIONAL EXPERIENCE

Through the experience related here, our narrator learned that the bond between two people can be strong enough to survive even death, and she came to discover the expanded horizons that can result once we realize that our existence is not limited to the physical body.

*   *   *

"On November 21, 1979, my father passed on. He was found on his bed, a bottle of nitroglycerin pills on the table beside him, and the police were notified. My parents had been separated all but one year of my life. In fact, I hadn't even seen my father for four or five years before his death. We had, however, been corresponding. Little did I realize what a bond still existed between us—stronger and more enduring than I ever imagined.

"The Sunday following my father's death, I sat with a pencil and paper, alone in my room, and I asked him to talk to me. We hadn't said good-bye. I felt there should at least be the chance to do so now.

"For two hours nothing happened. Then the pencil began to scribble—slowly and painstakingly at first. But gradually the writing grew in strength and urgency: 'COME TO MY HOUSE. COME TO MY HOUSE . . .' Not only did the script become more legible, but the words got larger and larger as the message went on.

"This incident began a venture for me into a broader, more expanded consciousness that, although a little unsettling at first, has now become as much a part of my being as breathing. It is merely another facet of my earthly experience.

"Some might think my contact was simply the result of grief; but I can say, from my own personal involvement, that it was not. I was not close enough to my father to grieve for him that deeply or feel such a devastating sense of loss. In fact, the only reason I found his death shocking at all was not that he was gone, but that I discovered he was still 'alive'!

"Over the years my contact with my father has tapered off, but it has not ended."   *C. P. P.*

Our final story of this chapter is a bit different from most of the others in that it shows the grief caused by the separation death brings. This feeling of sadness was probably deepened by the extremely strong, emotional attachment between my correspondent and her brother. But even here we can gain a sense of the comfort to be found in knowing that the dead continue to exist and that they can still feel and express love for us.

LOVE SENDS A MESSAGE

It seems that the experience described in this very human account reassured our contributor of some basic truths regarding the immortality of the soul. We can hope that in doing so it helped her cope with her sorrow.

"I received a cablegram with the sad news of my brother's sudden death. Just a few days before, he had visited me in New York City. At that time he had looked healthy and appeared to be very happy.

"The cable was a terrible shock. After my father had died when I was five years old, my brother had been the only male member of the family left. To me he had been both father and brother. When the news of his passing arrived, I locked myself in my room to cry. I could not be consoled.

"Suddenly I stopped crying. My brother stood in front of me, dressed in white! He looked very sad. I was afraid even to bat my eyes, for fear he would leave; but after a time he did—all too soon for me—disappear.

"Because of my belief in reincarnation, I feel my brother appeared to show me that there is no death of the soul—only of the body. And I believe he also came to tell me that he loved me, too, and that he would miss me as I missed him."   *M. R. F.*

Like all the stories in this chapter, the brother's implicit message underscores a theme: the transition into another form of life does *not* involve a loss of awareness or contact with the material plane. No doubt the experience of actually dying involves feelings and perceptions that are virtually impossible to describe adequately in language. But whatever the details of that experience may be like, nevertheless it is an *expansion* of consciousness, a broadening to include the spirit world *and* the physical world.

5

WHERE WE GO FROM HERE

THE STATE OF consciousness a soul experiences in the afterlife is beyond time or space, as we know those dimensions. This is part of what makes speculation about the nature of the spirit world so intriguing. The concept of higher dimensions of consciousness is fascinating, but it will be hard to satisfy our intellectual curiosity about these expanded levels of awareness. When Cayce was asked in readings to explain those realms—fourth, fifth, and higher dimensions—he gave just a few clues.

The fourth dimension he defined as the realm of ideas—that is, the state of consciousness in which thoughts are totally real and immediately perceived. This chapter will present considerable evidence for just how vivid this fourth-dimensional thought-world is to the recently departed. But beyond that hint, Cayce was not inclined to give information, saying simply that we have enough trouble understanding our own three-dimensional world.

Even though the afterlife is an expansion beyond time and space—as physical beings experience them—still, we can sometimes understand a deceased individual as "located" somewhere. In other words, that soul may focus its consciousness on a specific earth location. When its after-death spirit body is perceived as an apparition in a particular place, we usually call it a ghost.

But ghosts are not so mysterious or frightful once we understand that certain spiritual laws are at work.

A VERY PROPER GHOST

In this story, our narrator gives us a clear picture of the presence of a soul after death. The childhood vision of her deceased aunt includes an interesting feature. The propriety of the ghost's choice of wardrobe—presumably consistent with the aunt's behavior in physical life—is one of those interesting details that can help us view the dead as distinct, believable individuals.

"I am sixty-four-and-one-half years old. The experience I relate here took place approximately sixty years ago. I was four or five when my Aunt Marguerete died. She was about twenty-three years old at the time of her passing, and many an hour I had spent on her lap. She was my friend!

"Marguerete had lived with my grandmother, her mother. She had never married. But, like many girls, she had a trousseau, which she kept in a trunk at the foot of her bed. The trousseau included a white wedding gown. When Marguerete suddenly died, my mother took me to my grandmother's house, and we stayed there a week for the wake and funeral. There were no funeral parlors in those days, and Marguerete was laid out in the living room of that house. Before the coffin was brought in, she was lying on a bier, in a powder blue gown. Later she was dressed in her white wedding gown from the trousseau, placed in the coffin, and buried in that white dress.

"At my young age I witnessed all this.

"Three days after the funeral, while we were still at my grandmother's house, I was sleeping alongside my mother. I awoke early in the morning and noticed how light it was. The sun was rising. There was a grandfather's clock on the wall in the kitchen, so I slipped out of bed and scrambled downstairs. As I approached the kitchen, I could see that the clock indicated either five minutes to six or five after six.

"I walked into the kitchen. My Aunt Marguerete was sitting at the table, dressed in the powder blue gown she had worn on the bier. Her hands were in her lap and her head was bowed. But as I entered the kitchen, she slowly raised her head and our eyes met. An expression of amazement came over her face as she realized I could see her. We stared at each other for how long I do not know; but finally I broke away and ran upstairs into the bedroom, grabbed my mother's arm, and shook her awake.

" 'Aunt Marguerete's downstairs in the kitchen,' I said. My mother knew me well enough to know I was speaking the truth. She jumped out of that bed as if she were ejected by springs, grabbed me, and we both flew down the stairs. There was no one in the kitchen.

"We went back home that same day. I have never forgotten this incident. However, for a while I did wonder——Why was Marguerete dressed in the powder blue gown, instead of the white wedding gown she had been buried in? After a little thought, I realized the simple answer. Why should she wear a wedding gown, when there had never been a wedding? Freedom of choice is present to a degree, even in the afterlife."

                                                                    C. W. B.

In this incident, as in a number of other reported appearances, we find the ghost in the same home in which the person had lived during physical life. This could lead us to believe that after death the soul stays on in the same environs it had inhabited before. According to the picture that emerges from material I have received and from the Cayce readings, this is sometimes true up to a point——certain souls remain for a time in the surroundings that had been familiar to them in life. But, as we shall see, there is a somewhat more complex answer to the question of where we go when we leave the body behind.

BUILDING OUR OWN EXPERIENCES IN THE AFTERLIFE

The question of where we go when physical life is over is indeed a fascinating one. Do we move on to a classical heaven or hell? Do we indefinitely hang around the physical area where we had spent our lives, as many reported ghosts seem to do? Do we just slide into oblivion? Or is there some other experience waiting for us when we make the transition?

When asked in one reading about where we go, Edgar Cayce gave a simple and direct answer: To the place you are preparing and to what you individually are creatively building. (See reading 1219-1.)

Several passages from the readings describe death as merely a birth into a new experience. But what will that new experience be like? This depends entirely on what the soul has created for itself and for others. There is no single after-death experience that will be met by everyone. Through our individual actions, we ourselves build our own heaven or our own hell. What we choose to do with our lives, through the exercise of our God-given will, determines the condition we will pass into at death.

We reap what we have sown after death, just as we do in physical life. Each of us should ask ourselves, "What have I sown in life?" We all must live with ourselves and with what we have made of our opportunities. For example, as a statement of spiritual law the Cayce readings admonish us: never ask anyone to do something that might bring shame or disgrace to that soul. To do otherwise creates a difficulty for oneself that has to be met in the afterlife and probably a future earth life.

In considering just what kind of afterlife we are creating for ourselves, we must remember that we do not build with only our bodies. Perhaps the single most often repeated idea in all the Cayce material is "Mind is the builder." Many of the readings stress that the *results* of this creative power of the mind do not end with death. Our mental habits—our thoughts, our purposes and ideals, our intents and desires—are powerful molders of our lives, both in this world and in the next. What we believe, what we think about, and what we wish for ardently may be brought into our experience.

Our next two stories clearly illustrate how strongly our patterns of thought can affect what we will find at the end of physical life.

THE DROWNING GHOST

Some years ago I came across an account of a woman who had a repeated and troubling dream. Her story emphasizes two key points. First, it shows how our beliefs influence our experiences after death. What we think we will meet in the afterlife, we very well may! Second, the experience illustrates how a deceased soul can still be very conscious of conditions in material life, particularly something to which there was a strong attachment before death.

In her dreams, a woman saw a deceased relative begging her to move his casket. He kept saying, "I am drowning! I am drowning!" The dream was repeated night after night, and the woman could get little rest. Eventually she sought and was able to obtain permission for her relative's grave to be opened. To the great surprise of the people present, they found the coffin to be submerged in water! Needless to say, the coffin and the body it held were moved to higher ground. At that point, the disturbing dreams ceased.

This is an excellent example of what can occur when

a person believes he or she will simply remain in the casket after death. A problem such as this is particularly likely to persist if the soul has no one praying for it, since there will then be no positive influence to help it move beyond its self-imposed confinement.

SHE SLEPT FOR 700 YEARS

The experience of one of my friends shows how our desires concerning the afterlife can help determine what we meet when we die. As can be seen here, this does not always work out to the soul's advantage.

A woman friend of mine had a life reading from Edgar Cayce. One of the former incarnations that Cayce described took place at the time of the Crusades. During that lifetime, my friend had been a man with very high ideals. This man became disgusted with the actions of many of those who took part in the Holy Wars. As a result of this disillusionment, the soul vowed that it would not come back as a man again and that it would rest a long, long time before returning to this earth plane.

In the psychic reading from Cayce, my present-day friend was told that because of the vow she had taken during the Crusades period, she had slept for 700 years, and when she did return it was as a female. Now, in this life, she is a wonderful woman, but rather masculine, unmarried, and totally uninterested in men. As Cayce said, those who wish a lengthy rest following a physical life may remain unconscious a long, long time!

Stories like this one make it hard to doubt the truth of Edgar Cayce's statement that with our thoughts and actions we build our own experiences after death. But still, there are certain patterns in the reports I have received which suggest that many souls go through typical *phases of spiritual development* between the close of one physical incarnation and the beginning of the next. These stages include (1) a period of unconsciousness and/or disorientation, (2) a time of healing and awakening, (3) an interval of activity as a spirit still close to the earth plane, and (4) a period of existence in nonearthly dimensions. Do keep in mind that none of these experiences are foreordained. It is our own choices that determine which stages we go through after death, how long we remain in each one, and the specific circumstances we meet on the other side.

The story of my friend who slept for 700 years gives an extreme example of something mentioned earlier— the period of unconsciousness through which a recently departed soul often goes. In Cayce's own words: "Passing from the material consciousness to a spiritual . . . consciousness, oft does an entity or being not become conscious of that [which is] about it . . ." (5749-3) As was the case with my friend, this stage can be prolonged by the soul's desire for extended rest. And, the Cayce readings tell us, the same effect can occur when a person does not believe in life after death. The soul that does not expect to awaken on the other side can take a long time to do so.

Another stage many souls experience after crossing over is an interval of confusion. It can take time for the soul to grasp what has happened to it and adjust to its new surroundings. When my own mother made the transition, I saw in my dream experiences that she went through periods of both unconsciousness and disorientation.

MY MOTHER'S EXPERIENCES AFTER DEATH

My mother's story has one feature that many people would find surprising: the soul's continued need for care and healing after death. The persistence of this need is what makes praying for the departed so very important.

When my mother was in her forties, she developed cancer. Being a registered nurse, I was able to look after her in the hospital. After a month or so, my mother passed on, at the age of only forty-five.

In my dreams, however, I was still taking care of her in a hospital on the other side, even though I continued to know she was physically dead. During these experiences I often said to her, "Mama, I know you are dead and my body is asleep in New York."

The cause of illness is in the soul, and it, too, needs to be healed. For example, the Cayce readings tell us that cancer can be caused by deep-seated resentment, whether brought on by an event in the current lifetime or one from a previous incarnation. My mother had been forced to marry the man of her parents' choice, although she loved another. What's more, in the latter part of her life, she discovered something that brought great resentment to her. I believe that this affected her soul and produced the cancer that followed. The deeper problem within her soul remained, even after the demise of her physical body.

In April of 1967, some time after my mother's death, I dreamed that she returned home and went up a special staircase. She stopped at a door, hesitated, and then went on up to a second one. She appeared to be slightly confused, and she was not sure where her apartment was located. I took her back to the first door, but she was unable to get it open. I then took the key and opened the door. We went in, and she seemed to be familiar with the place.

I interpreted this dream in accordance with Edgar Cayce's statement that a recently deceased person, having left the material body and the conscious mind behind, is sometimes similar to a newly born baby. The soul finds itself in strange surroundings, and at times it becomes disoriented and confused. This is another stage in which the prayers of the living can be of great help. How pronounced the confusion is and how long it lasts depend largely on the person's belief about life after death. Here, again, we find that what we believe colors our experiences in the life beyond.

Several of the reports my correspondents have sent me mention the same need for healing after death that my mother experienced. By way of explanation, the Cayce readings tell us that the familiar body of flesh and blood is not the only one the soul inhabits during the various stages of its development. When the material body passes away, the soul will have a different body to use, specifically suited to its existence on the other side. Like the material body, this other vehicle is influenced by the choices the soul makes. Thus our decisions affect not only the body that is ours during physical life, but the one we will inhabit after the transition as well. What we build with the mind—whether it be health or disease—lives on in our experiences even in the afterlife.

Some people might find it a bit depressing to think that they could continue to be sick even after they die. But there is no call for despair. As a number of the stories I have received show, departed souls in need of healing are able to find it in the afterlife, and help is available from several sources. As I have mentioned, the prayers of the living can be of great benefit to the deceased. In addition, the next world has places of convalescence for them. These points are illustrated in the following account:

PRAYERS ARE APPRECIATED

The man who sent me this report has contributed several other examples to this book. Perhaps his large number of contacts with the deceased is due in part to his active, wide-ranging prayer life. In this story, he introduces us to a soul in a stage of partial awakening.

*   *   *

"My first dream of contact with souls who had passed on came to me in 1972 or thereabouts, after the Cayce readings had made me aware of the importance of praying for the dead. For some time I had been interceding for deceased members of my family, and I decided to pray as well for my departed friends, most of whom were people I had known in childhood. So, on Christmas Eve, before falling asleep I prayed ardently for all of them.

"In a dream, I soon found myself with all those for whom I had prayed. We were extremely happy to see one another. We spent what seemed to be the better part of a day taking in the 'sights.' My friends were showing me the large 'city' in which they lived.

"Toward evening one person said to me, 'Warren, there is someone here who is most anxious to meet you.' With that I was taken to what appeared to be a huge convalescent home or hospital. We entered a large room and I was taken to see an elderly woman who seemed to be in some sort of sleep state. She was seated in a big, overstuffed chair, unable to speak. But she looked up at me and smiled. I awoke feeling very curious as to her identity.

"Some time before having this dream, I had asked my superior at work for her mother's birth date, without telling her why I wanted this information. I knew the mother was to have major surgery, and shortly after the operation she passed on.

"After my Christmas dream, I asked my superior if she had any photos of her mother. She said that she did, and the following day she brought one in to work. I was not really expecting to find my 'dream lady' that easily; but imagine my surprise, on seeing the picture of my superior's mother, to recognize the woman in my dreams!"   *W. W.*

If there are hospitals in the afterlife, what about doctors? Our next report indicates that they, too, are to be found on the other side and that they take an active role in bringing healing to the departed. We are not told whether they make house calls!

MORE HEALING FOR THE DECEASED

This account was contributed by the same source as the preceding story. Its last sentence tells us that personal contact with physicians in the next world can help the deceased along the road to recovery.

"A later contact with departed souls occurred in 1977. For at least two years before then, I had traveled to work in a carpool with two other men. One of them, named Dick, suffered from gout and certain other infirmities. I tried to interest him in the Cayce material, but to no avail. Some time later, he passed on.

"About six months after Dick died, I met him in a dream. Displaying no emotion whatsoever, we shook hands. I asked him how things were going. As if to reassure me, he introduced me to a man who was with him, saying, 'Warren, this is Dr.———. He is taking care of me, and everything is now all right.' "   *W. W.*

In this life, some of us need and receive healing for our bodies; others need help and guidance to improve their mental outlook. The same is true in the afterlife. Our last few stories have described physical-type healings on the other side. In our next account, we see a departed soul receiving support and undergoing experiences that will help bring about a healing of the mind, an adjustment of attitudes and emotions. The dramatic improvement that takes place can be extremely encouraging to all of us, for it shows that we will not be forever stuck with the mental and emotional shortcomings that are ours at the time of death.

SOUL GROWTH IN THE BEYOND

Our narrator has given us here a picture of a setting remarkable for its peacefulness and beauty, along with a very powerful statement of the need for prayer and the benefits it can bring.

"The relationship among my husband, his mother, and me had been very destructive. I'd met my mother-in-law just once before my marriage floundered, and I found her to be a most unhappy woman, full of bitterness and animosity. I did not see her again, nor did I have any further communication with her before she passed on ten years later.

"At the time of my mother-in-law's final serious illness, I obtained a psychic reading. Though my marriage of twenty years was in trouble at this point, the problem for which I sought the psychic help was totally unrelated to my husband or his mother. But to my surprise, the mystic identified the detrimental situation among the three of us, which had seemingly existed for numerous lifetimes. She urged me to pray very hard to dissolve the negativity, and she warned me severely that if I did not take the initiative in this matter, we would be condemned to repeat this unhappy cycle in the future!

"I followed her advice very seriously for many months, through the summer and fall of that year. I worked daily at prayer, asking for a loving relationship among the three of us. The following spring I learned that my mother-in-law had passed on, but I continued to pray for her.

"One day after my prayers, I suddenly found myself in a beautiful park with sunlit lawns and flower-filled gardens. My mother-in-law was weeding a flower bed, and I knew she was at peace and happy. As I watched, my father, who had passed on more than thirty years before, walked across the lawn to speak to her.

"I understood that I had seen her soul at peace, and I was granted the additional joy of knowing that my father had been one of her welcomers and continued to be her loving companion. In this last lifetime they had not known each other, but it's possible they had been friends during other incarnations. Or perhaps my father had been there simply to help me. No matter. I knew with a certainty that my mother-in-law's spirit was being cleansed and healed in an environment of love and beauty."

P. H.

Several aspects of the soul's healing after death are mentioned in a reading Edgar Cayce gave for a young woman who fell from her dormitory window at college and was killed. After assuring the people close to the student that her death was not a suicide, Cayce spoke of the awakening of the soul on the other side, its growth in understanding of what happened to it, and the mending of the body it inhabited in the afterlife. There is also included a clear affirmation of the power of prayer to help those who have passed on.

A DEPARTED SOUL'S RECOVERY

In requesting this reading from Edgar Cayce, the young woman's loved ones asked to receive any helpful information available. The questions at the end were posed by her aunt, who was present for the reading. This rather short reading is of such relevance to our study of the afterlife that I've included it here in its entirety.

Mr. Cayce: Yes, we are with the entity here.

This, as may be and should be understood by those who are interested, was an accident—and not premeditated or purposed by the entity.

The environs or surroundings that made for these

happenings, in a material world, are with the entity in the present, making for better understandings.

Those that are near and dear to the entity, to make for more understandings—condemn no one, nor the circumstance. Neither mourn for those that are at rest.

There is gradually coming the awakening. This, to be sure, is an experience through which the entity . . . is passing in the present. It is making for a helpfulness in its understanding and comprehending of that which is the experience, the awareness of same in the present.

The body-physical that was broken is now whole in Him.

Let thy prayer then be:

"IN THY MERCY, IN THY GOODNESS, FATHER, KEEP HER. MAKE FOR THOSE UNDERSTANDINGS IN MY EXPERIENCE, IN HER EXPERIENCE, THAT WE MAY DRAW NEARER AND NEARER TOGETHER IN THAT ONENESS OF PURPOSE THAT HIS LOVE IS KNOWN MORE AND MORE IN THE MINDS AND THE HEARTS OF THOSE THAT ARE IN THE POSITIONS OF OPPORTUNITIES FOR BEING A CHANNEL, A MESSENGER, IN THE NAME OF THE CHRIST. AMEN."

Ready for questions.

Q. Is she happy, and does she understand where she is?
A. As given, there is the awakening, and there is the understanding coming more and more.

And soon to the aunt may come the awareness of her presence near.

These are the conditions.

Q. Is there anything any of us can do to help her in any way?
A. Let the prayer as given be held occasionally, especially in the early mornings.

We are through with this reading.   4938-1

EXPERIENCES OF THE DEAD IN THE EARTH PLANE

After the death of the body, the soul typically remains about the earth for a period of time. Here it goes through any phases of unconsciousness, confusion, and recovery appropriate to its individual development. Once consciousness is regained, the soul can become active in and about the earth. It is during this stage of earthly activity that those in the spirit world are able to communicate with the living. One Cayce reading—3744-2—indicated that souls who have passed on remain about the physical plane until their development carries them onward or they reincarnate for their development. When they are disembodied but still near the physical plane, they may be communicated with. In that particular reading, Cayce stated that there were "thousands about us here at present."

This concept helps us put the earth-connected phase of the soul's experiences after death in perspective. From that part of the spirit world that is vibrationally close to the earth plane, the soul will eventually travel in one of two directions: it can move on to spiritual experiences in other realms, or it can return to physical incarnation in another material body. Before the soul takes either of these paths, contact with the living is possible. As the following account of my mother's final message to me shows, such communication comes to an end when the soul is about to be reborn into another physical life.

A SOUL'S LOVING GOOD-BYE

My final contact with my mother told me that she had reached the point in her spiritual development where her soul would benefit from another experience in physical life. It also reassured me of her continuing love. About thirty years after her death, my mother came to me while I was in a semi-conscious state. She kissed me on the cheek and said, in German, "I've come to say good-bye, my child. For I am about to be reborn and I will not be seeing you again."

I never again had contact with my mother, in a dream or otherwise, following this disclosure of her coming rebirth.

Of course, in our daily interpersonal relations in life, we cannot always communicate with whomever we would like. The other person might not be available, or he or she might not want to speak with us. The same is true regarding souls who have passed on. Communication with them does not happen automatically. For us to establish contact with the departed, they must be in the earth plane, where they are available to us. And they must be willing for the contact to take place. The presence of departed souls about the earth and their desire for contact with the living is shown in our next two reports. In each case, the purpose of the communication was evidently to offer encouragement and comfort to loved ones who were left behind.

COMFORT FROM A DECEASED FATHER

Here a parent returns to offer my correspondent reassurance about a difficult decision. In doing so, he demonstrates that his concern for his child lives on and that the deceased generally have a sound reason for their efforts to communicate with us.

"In 1971 I left the home of my parents. My childhood had not been a very happy one. Two weeks after I moved out, my father died of a heart attack. He passed on just as my mother was about to leave for work one morning. She was especially distraught because they had argued the night before.

"I showed no emotion at the funeral. In the days following the service, my mother put a great deal of pressure on me to return home. She was now all alone, and she didn't want to stay in the house by herself, particularly because my father had died in their bedroom. I really felt guilty, since I thought it was my responsibility to move back in with her; but I couldn't go back and lose what I wanted and needed so much—my freedom.

"One work night about two weeks after the funeral, I was sleeping in the bedroom of my new apartment. Being broke, I could afford only two pictures, like posters backed by cardboard, to cover the walls in the room. They were huge—about two-and-one-half feet wide by three-and-one-half feet long. At 2:10 a.m. (I can be sure of the time because I had a digital clock near my bed) both posters fell off the wall at the same time and crashed to the floor. I sat up in bed, looked at the clock, and then glanced at the front door.

"The apartment was dark, but I could see my father standing at the door in the bathrobe he often wore. He assured me that he was fine, and he asked me if I was all right and what I was doing that weekend. He tried to comfort me about my decision not to move back home. Then he told me he loved me and said to take care.

"It was a very casual and loving conversation. I don't remember speaking, so I'm pretty sure our communication was telepathic. When it was over, I realized I had not even been frightened. I couldn't believe how calm I had been, because at that time in my life I was really afraid of the dark and any type of psychic occurrence. But it had seemed so natural just to be talking to my father, who was dead.

"My sister and her husband, who lived in the apartment downstairs, had no such experience."   *L. D.*

A POSSIBLE POLTERGEIST
EXPERIENCE

This story, contributed by the same person as the one above, may represent a similar desire on the part of the deceased to comfort the living. It, too, shows that the departed can put a certain amount of physical energy into their efforts to get in touch with us.

"My second experience occurred one day last summer while I was with two friends in the cellar of the house where one of them lived. We had been talking for a couple of hours, having an interesting discussion about sex, and drinking to keep cool. Right in the middle of our conversation, the backs of two pictures fell out of their frames at the same time, causing the frames and the glass to break. The photos were of my friend's two children, one of whom was in the armed services and in uniform.

"While this was happening, my friend stared at me in amazement, not knowing what to do. She asked me if something might be wrong with her son and whether I thought the pictures' falling was some kind of sign. I tried to reassure her, but I felt a lot of energy in the air.

"The next day my mother called to tell me that my uncle had died the day the pictures fell. At the funeral I told my uncle's daughter of the experience. Since this sort of thing had happened to me before, I thought it might be my uncle's way of letting his daughter know that he was O.K."   *L. D.*

Good conversationalists generally spend part of the time speaking, part listening. There are some things they want to say to their partners, and some they'd like to hear from them. The dead can follow the same rules of a good relationship. We have just seen several accounts in which they contacted the living in order to give some message to them. Our next two stories show the other side of the coin—the desire of the deceased to communicate with those in physical life so that they can learn from us.

AN INVITATION

In this amusing story, we meet a soul desiring to obtain information and guidance from the living. I was quite taken by the casual way my correspondent's aunt expresses this wish—"When are you coming over . . . ?"

"In one of my dreams I communicated with an aunt who had died in 1947. My aunt suddenly appeared before me and said, 'Boy, Warren, did I have a hard time getting through to you!' This startled me so that I was stunned into silence.

"My aunt then asked, 'When are you coming over to teach us?' This startled me even more, as I was fully aware that she was dead!

"I replied, 'I'll be over one of these days.' It seemed to be understood between us that I was to teach them about Jesus and the Cayce material.

"Apparently my answer satisfied her, for she said, 'O.K.' And she was gone as quickly as she had come."

W. W.

The above account shows that, at least in some cases, the dead can learn useful lessons from the living. This leads us to a very important point: Making the transition does not automatically give a soul unlimited wisdom. The same concept is illustrated in our following story. Here again we can see souls who still inhabit the earth plane coming into contact with the living for the sake of the lessons they can gain.

GHOSTS ATTEND A LECTURE

Edgar Cayce once told my husband Bill and me this brief but fascinating story. It raises an interesting possibility: even at times when we're not aware of it, those on the other side of life may be in contact with us.

Edgar Cayce had an unusual experience one stormy night when he was scheduled to give a lecture. The setting was a vacant store that had been converted into a meeting hall. It was raining so hard that only a few friends and family members were there.

Mr. Cayce was about to cancel his talk when he clairvoyantly saw people from the other side of life file into the hall until almost every chair was taken. This convinced him to go ahead with his address. Those few members of the audience who were still in physical life said later that his talk that night was the most inspiring they had ever heard him give.

So if you're ever speaking in public, don't be dismayed if the hall isn't full. Ghosts may be there!

A JOYFUL MEETING

The Cayce readings tell us that the souls of people who have departed physical life remain about the earth until their development takes them elsewhere. Several of the reports I have received support this idea that eventually the dead move onward from their nonmaterial activities around our planet. The following story of a happy reunion is a good example, showing that the souls of the dead are not all in the same place. My correspondent's deceased mother was still about the earth plane and so was able to communicate with her son. But his deceased father had evidently moved beyond, and thus was not available to either the son or the mother.

*   *   *

"In this dream of contact, which came in 1973 or 1974, I saw my mother, who had died about seven or eight years before. 'Oh, Mom,' I said, 'it's really you!' We embraced, and it was a very happy moment for me.

"Then she said, 'I can't find your father. I've searched and searched for him, but I can't find him.'

"I said, 'Mom, he has probably already moved on to another plane of existence.'

"She seemed to understand, and in a few moments her 'bus' arrived. We kissed each other and said good-bye. She then got on the bus and departed."   *W. W.*

Stories like this, which show that souls move away from the earth for certain stages in their development, naturally make us stop and wonder just where does the development carry the soul onward. Several passages in the Edgar Cayce material tell us about these nonearthly realms which the soul can come to inhabit. In one such reading, Cayce says that in death we merely "pass from one room to another" of God's great universe. (2282-1)

These "rooms," the destinations of souls leaving the earth plane, are states of consciousness associated with the other planets of our solar system. Each of these states is a step along the way to the expanded consciousness God would have each of us reach and express in our relationships with others.

Another reading (541-1) explains that each nonearthly realm has distinct characteristics of its own. Therefore, each has a specific, necessary contribution to make to spiritual growth. When the time comes for the soul of the deceased to leave the earth, it is attracted to the planetary environment most suited to its individual stage of development.

Does this mean that when physical travel to our neighboring planets becomes possible, we will be greeted there by our dead relatives, walking around in little green bodies? An interesting idea, and to some people perhaps an appealing one. But according to the Cayce readings, it will not turn out that way. In speaking of our solar system, Cayce specifically states that "only upon the earth plane at present do we find man is flesh and blood . . ." (3744-3) Cayce associates the nonearthly planes in our system with states of consciousness needed for the nonmaterial aspects of soul growth.

What can we expect to happen as the soul leaves the earth plane for the nonearthly realms? In one respect, that change could be similar to physical death. The Cayce readings tell us that a soul is composed of a body-physical; a body-mental; and a body-soul, or body-spiritual. The body-soul is an inhabitant of that dimension we call heaven. The body-mental is our vehicle of experience for many of the after-death realms. The body-physical is a citizen of that which we now call home, this earth.

Each of these "bodies" is appropriate for its own realm. When the soul departs one dimension for another, it leaves behind the body suited to the old residence. Just as a soul whose physical life has ended leaves its material body behind, one that is moving beyond the nonmaterial phase of its activities in the earth leaves the body it had inhabited in that domain of which it no longer has need.

Here is the explanation for an interesting phenomenon once observed by an individual who had left the physical body and visited the nonmaterial side of the earth plane. After this adventure, the person asked Mr. Cayce why some beings seen in the nonmaterial plane were animated, while others appeared to be waxen images.

In his reply, Cayce identified the images as "shells," each one being ". . . the body of an individual that has been left when its soul self has projected on" to other dimensions. (516-4) These shells might be compared to the ashes that remain in the physical world after the cremation of the material body. The ones that the inquirer had seen had not yet dissolved into the astral realm. The animated beings, on the other hand, were individuals who were still actively experiencing existence in the nonmaterial phase of the earth plane.

The soul's passage from the earth sphere to other realms is the subject of our next story. Here we can see that, like physical death itself, this move from one spirit plane to another is not a haphazard event; it is something for which the soul prepares. If my correspondent is correct in interpreting this incident as a farewell message, this account supports the idea that the normal period of communication with departed souls lasts for as long as they remain about the earth.

A TRIP ON "THE RIVER OF LIFE"

This report was contributed by the same person who gave us the account in Chapter 3 of a friend's prophetic dream about his deceased father and his neighbor Ike. Though the activity described here is somewhat different, the feeling tone of this story is similar to my mother's farewell visit to me.

"My friend had another dream of contact with his deceased father. In this experience my friend's dad told him that he was going on a boat trip up a river. My friend's father then took him to a wharf and showed him a new canoe that he said he had just built.

"My friend looked at the canoe and told his father that it did not seem to have been varnished. His dad smiled and said, 'Take a closer look.' When my friend did this, he found that the canoe had in fact been varnished, with a very good type of finish that was hardly visible to the naked eye.

"My interpretation of this dream was that my friend's father was about to move to another plane of existence and that he was really prepared for this trip. When he got to his new dimension, communication with his son might no longer be possible, and so he had made this last visit to say good-bye.

"As far as I know, my friend never had another contact with his dad."

W. J. W.

The concluding story for this chapter contains a more explicit message of farewell. Like the preceding one, it shows a soul who is prepared to move from one spiritual dimension to the next. An interesting point is that in this case the soul holds out hope that future contact may still be possible even after he has moved on. Perhaps this shows an ability to return in cases of emergency from the nonearthly spheres back to the spiritual side of the earth plane. This report also gives us a vivid sense of the soul's need to progress and develop on the other side, and it demonstrates that this need can be strong enough to override a dear daughter's grief.

A BELOVED PARENT MOVES ON

The woman who gave us this story had had two earlier experiences with her deceased father, which are related in Chapter 7. In this moving account, her father's concern for her is obvious, as is the importance of this contact to her. Quite possibly it was this communication, painful though it was to receive, that enabled my correspondent to close her report with an affirmation of faith.

"My third dream of contact with my deceased father was different from the first two. In this one, I was totally aware of what was going on, and I did not have to wake up to understand its meaning. This dream occurred about two years after Daddy's death.

"In the dream, I was walking down a path through

the woods in a mountain area. I saw Daddy up ahead on the path, waiting for me. I ran up to him, full of joy at seeing him. I noticed he was dressed for hiking. He had on jeans, a flannel shirt, boots, and a backpack—a costume I'm sure he never wore when he was physically alive.

. "I said to him, 'You're going away!' And I knew that he was.

"I then behaved so badly that later when I awakened I was embarrassed. In the dream I cried and cried and begged him not to leave. I carried on for a long time with an abandon that I have never experienced while awake.

"Through all my distress, Daddy was calm, loving, and comforting; but he left no doubt in my mind what the outcome was going to be. He made me understand that if I really needed him he would be available, and that in times of great grief, hardship, or sorrow he would be with me.

"My sobbing awakened me, and I continued to weep for a very long time.

"When my father had left this physical life, I had been proud of the way I had given the appearance of handling his death. But the truth was that I had been nearly comatose! I missed him terribly and was almost overcome with grief. In fact, I had not coped with his death at all.

"And so, my first contacts with Daddy after his passing had brought me great joy and comfort. By the time of this third dream, I had come to feel that he was a part of my everyday life. Our communication in these dreams seemed so normal. I never heard my father speak in any of them, but I always knew what he wanted to tell me.

"I feel that he appeared to me in this dream because he understood that I had not truly dealt with his passing. I know that he did not want just to move on and leave me to wonder why he was no longer present when I thought about him or called him. If Daddy hadn't come to me in that last dream, I probably would have become ill or depressed and not understood why.

"Now I know there is no death of the soul!"

B. L. D.

6

WHO WE ARE AFTER DEATH

ANYONE WHO THINKS about the afterlife surely wonders just how much his or her own consciousness will be transformed by shedding the physical body. "Will I still be me—the person I know myself to be?" On the one hand we can expect to retain our personalities, according to the Cayce readings and the diverse stories I have collected. At least for a substantial period after death, our likes and dislikes are carried over. Our interests and aspirations continue. At the same time, there can be an expansion of who we know ourselves to be. We can become aware of a wider perspective of the meaning of life. In the language that Edgar Cayce used, we could say that the personality continues after death, but at the same time there is likely to be an awakening of individuality—the identity of the soul.

A MATTER OF PRIDE

In this story we meet a soul who expresses concern over a totally commonplace matter. This is one of the features that make this account so believable. Being able to wear shoes had been important to our narrator's mother before her death; it continued to be important to her afterward. Here is a clear illustration of how the personality identity survives.

*   *.   *

"My daughter, who is now twenty-two years old and married, has had several psychic dreams and premonitions, particularly during her teen years. One very interesting and unusual dream experience came to her after my mother's death in March of 1982. My daughter may have forgotten this experience, but it meant a lot to me, for it confirmed that there is life after death.

"In the dream, my deceased mother told my daughter to inform me that I had done an excellent job with the funeral and its preparations. However, she did not like being buried without shoes, and there were some that would have fit if only I had looked for them a little harder!

"My mother had had edema prior to her death, and she had been very upset that no decent shoes would fit her. In fact, I remember buying a very large size just so she might be able to slip them on. She was barely able to walk in them, but having suitable shoes helped her self-esteem. After her passing, a relative and I had tried in vain to find a fitting and matching pair for her. But, as her later appearance to my daughter showed, her footwear was a matter of pride to her, and she found being buried without shoes devastating!"   *I. Y.*

This story graphically shows that after death the deceased is still basically the same person he or she was before. This fact can be seen in the desires, interests, and concerns which departed souls communicate to the living. It is manifested as well in the memories, emotions, attitudes, and beliefs they retain following their transition. And, in some cases, it is shown even in their activities on the other side.

Throughout the earlier chapters, we have seen considerable evidence that we continue to exist after physical death. In this chapter we will go one step beyond this basic truth and see that we survive death, not just as members of the human race, but as individuals with distinct personalities. In other words, in order to get an idea of who you are likely to be *after* death, start by looking at the person you are *now*. Our next story makes this point most strongly. It does not involve contact with a soul in the spirit world, but instead this account describes how one person's dreams gave a detailed lesson about the nature of the after-death state.

A POSSIBLE PREMONITION

This description of what it might be like to be dead clearly affirms that individual memories and emotions live on. In all the elements of my correspondent's personality, death causes only a single change.

"In a dream I was on board an airplane, and we were taking off. After a few moments I heard a loud noise, followed by a terrible vibration in the rear of the plane. We started to dive, and people were screaming in terror. I turned to the man beside me, patted his leg, and tried to calm him by telling him we would be all right, even if we were killed. I was unexcited until it occurred to me that I might not die, but be badly hurt and suffer greatly instead.

"As we impacted and before I was hurt, I saw my soul leave my body. At that point all motion seemed to stop. I realized what had happened and called to my disembodied self in order to see what it looked like. By will power I turned it to face me. It looked exactly like me.

"Wanting very much to know what lives on after death, I passed through this disembodied or soul self, stopping long enough to merge consciousness in some way. I realized that almost nothing was lost! This self had my memory—even down to my address and phone number. My emotions and everything about me, except for the survival instinct, was the same. To describe this difference better, my soul had no fear of injury, illness, or death; it had none of the many emotions tied to such an experience. After making this discovery, I awoke.

"Three days later a DC-10 crashed on takeoff in Chicago, killing almost all those on board. I knew this was the crash I had experienced in my dream."   *H. G.*

The following account of a nighttime visitation illustrates some of the same concepts as the previous report. The soul's memory of her quilting projects and her interest in that hobby have survived her transition. So has her fondness for social visiting. From what we are told here, it would seem that death has changed this woman's personality very little, if at all.

A VISIT FROM ANOTHER WORLD

This story is appealing in the complete naturalness of the dream conversation between my correspondent and her mother. We can easily imagine that many mothers and daughters might talk about the same things in the same way. The only difference is that here one of the participants is dead.

"A number of women and children seemed to be going noisily into and out of my room. I said, 'Close that door.' I wanted to sleep. One of the people kept her back half-turned to me and stood at the far side of my bed, near the head. I knew it was Mama.

"I felt happy, but so surprised. I said, 'What are you doing here? You can't be here. You are . . .'

"Before I could say 'dead,' she said, 'I can go anywhere I want to. I am free to go wherever I want.'

"I realized that I could ask her anything, and she would answer me. I also knew that to continue our conversation I must stay in my dream state. I asked, 'What do you do all day?'

"By this time she was at the foot of the bed. Another

woman, whose face came into focus more sharply than Mama's, stood beside her and looked straight at me. Mama glanced at the other woman, laughed, and said, 'I talk a lot.' Of course, I thought—she always liked to visit.

"Then she said, 'I believe I made that quilt on your bed.' In fact, she had—a red and white flower-garden pattern.

"I said, 'You certainly did. You made lots of quilts, didn't you? I expect you made thirty.' She said, rather smugly, 'More like a hundred.' The dream ended here, perhaps because I went into a deeper sleep. I think the other woman was a sister of mine who had died in 1948 at age twenty. She looked so intently at me that I felt I should know her. This woman appeared to be thirty or thirty-five, and she was wearing a robe-type dress similar to one I have seen worn by Mary, the mother of Jesus. I wish I had talked to her; it seems they waited for me to initiate the conversation."   *L. S.*

Though our next story takes us on a much wider-ranging journey, it exhibits the same natural quality and the same continuance of personality traits as does the preceding one. An interesting sidelight to this report is the change of age noted in the deceased, who appeared younger than he had been at death. Edgar Cayce stated that whereas in this dimension we grow older, on the other side of life the old grow younger. Only the very young mature. Generally, fifty years of age is considered the ideal in that realm.

Cayce once explained this phenomenon to a person who asked, "Why did I see my father and his two brothers as young men, although I knew them when they were white-haired?"

His answer: "They are growing, as it were, upon the eternal plane. For, as may be experienced in every entity, a death is a birth. And those that are growing then appear in their growing state." (516-4) In other words, they are re-experiencing youth, the state in which growth naturally occurs.

A VISIT TO ANOTHER WORLD

In this account the departed soul's eagerness to show my correspondent his new place of residence, and their casual hillside chat, show the endurance of a close, easy-going friendship that the two must have shared while both were alive.

"H. K., a close friend of mine, died quite suddenly a little over a year ago at the age of forty-nine. Shortly after his death I had a dream in which I saw him very clearly, and he looked like a man in his twenties.

"In the dream, H. K. was showing me around his world. He told me that I probably wouldn't remember all the places he took me to. He was a captain in the navy, and I noticed that people around him were calling him 'Captain.' I recall his talking to a number of 'professors,' but I couldn't quite understand what he was saying to them. It seems to me that he was showing me 'reflections' or something to that effect. Things were similar to the earth plane, though I remember feeling it was kind of cold.

"We sat down on a hillside or in a landscape-type scene, and we talked and laughed as we always used to do. I asked him if he had planned on dying, and he said, 'No, but I'm getting along all right.'

"When I awoke, I was aware of the feeling that I had been awake the whole time, passing from the dream state to my normal waking consciousness. It seems that H. K. showed me many places in that world; but, as he had said, when the experience was over I didn't remember much of it. I do know that for some reason showing me the place where he had gone was important to him. He seemed to be a little confused in his new surroundings, but he was adjusting. I realize that this is rather vague, but that's the impression with which I was left."

R. J. G.

A similar sense of comfortable communication between friends is present in our next story. It is interesting that in this case the deceased shows no trace of the confusion or unconsciousness many of the recently departed may experience. Perhaps this is because of his animated nature. We have seen that a person who wants only to rest after death can remain unconscious for an extremely long time; it is reasonable that one full of enthusiasm and eager to get on with its new adventure on the other side of life would be up and going very quickly.

A FRIEND ATTENDS HIS OWN FUNERAL

In this story our narrator introduces us to a soul brimming over with enthusiasm and vitality—traits the person may well have possessed during physical life. It would be hard to imagine a more powerful illustration that the dead continue to live; as we see here, they can be very lively indeed.

"H. L. was a man I greatly admired. Although I had dreamed about him before meeting him in Virginia Beach, I had not been particularly drawn to him at that time. But when I met him a few years later in Hawaii, I found him very appealing. After half an hour's conversation, I felt as if we had been close all our lives. At subsequent meetings here in Hawaii and in Virginia Beach, we enjoyed each other's company, talked freely, and shared confidences. I felt as close to him as to many of my friends I had known for years. I prayed for him daily after his kidney surgery and have continued to do so since his passing.

"Several days following his demise, H. L. came to me in a dream and we chatted on and on like two children. He was excited and his voice high-pitched. He told me of all the things he thought we had in common. I knew he was wrong, since I didn't have his qualities, but I was ashamed to say so.

"H. L. was very excited about his coming memorial service and asked me to attend. I went with him to a far-off place. There he met several relatives and old friends. He seemed more animated than ever!

"They all sat along a back wall on a ledge, a bench, or chairs, with windows behind them. I watched this from a distance, as there was no seat for me in that section. The back of the room was L-shaped, and I sat on the side. H. L. and his friends could see the ceremony, but from where I sat I could see only them. I could neither see nor hear the memorial. Everyone sitting along the windows in the back was so happy for H. L.; however, he himself seemed to be totally engrossed in the service."
                                                        H. G.

LOVE SURVIVES BEYOND THE GRAVE

Our individuality survives death in ways other than simply the personality traits we retain after the transition. It also lives on in our continued affection for those close to us. Much of my correspondence conveys the encouraging message that love endures beyond the demise of the body. The people who are dear to us in physical life remain dear to us in death.

The survival of love can be seen in the following report. This account may be a description of a past-life recollection, a premonition of death in the future, a current out-of-body experience, or a simple representation of what it is like to die. But in any case, real concern for loved ones is shown in my correspondent's wish to avoid scaring his child and in his concern over easing his wife's pain. His desire to comfort her and tell her he was all right is so like the feelings expressed in many of our other stories that we can take it to be a common part of the death experience.

AN EXPERIENCE OF DEATH

This report was contributed by the same man who gave us the preceding account and the one about the airplane crash. Here we have a clear picture of the survival of individuality and affection.

"Another experience in which I 'died' also occurred in a dream. At the beginning of this one, I was attending a sporting event and sitting in the bleachers. A man who arrived late told me he had just visited with the Lord. The Lord had told him it was my time to die.

"I said, 'No, I won't accept that,' and I began to run. I ran and ran and ran, and finally I arrived home.

"Once home, safe and sound, I felt I had escaped and would be fine for the time being. I went to my room and sat on the edge of my bed to take off my shoes, as I usually do when I come home. At that point I felt a pain in my chest. I knew then that I hadn't escaped at all.

"I called one of my children and—not wanting to frighten him—told him very quietly to get his mom for me. I wanted to see her before I left. As I sat there, the pain got worse, and I realized that the child had gotten sidetracked and forgotten my request.

"I decided at that moment it was useless to fight any longer. I gave in and started to fall, but before I hit the ground my legs jerked. I kept my eyes open, as I didn't want to lose consciousness and miss what was going to happen. As my legs jerked, they somehow threw my disembodied self out through the bottom of my feet. I was surprised and soon found myself floating upside down in my room. I became embarrassed, thinking how foolish I must appear and that a disembodied soul should look more dignified, so I turned myself right-side up.

"I was concerned for my wife and didn't want her to suffer grief. So I went to her in the kitchen and tried to tell her I was O.K., but she didn't hear me. I felt that if I shouted loudly enough I would impress upon her mind that I was all right. I wanted to stay with her long enough to make sure this message got through and to protect her in any way I could. But there was some impelling force pulling at me and I had to follow it, so I left." *H. G.*

Our next story is of further appearances of Artie, whose earliest comforting visit to his wife was recounted in Chapter 1. Here we can see once again that he still cares for the same people who were important to him in physical life. His continuing love is clearly visible in his desire to be at his mother's birthday celebration; in the care he gives his granddaughter on the other side, and the impulse to tell those left behind that she is all right; and in his being there for his wife when she needed reassurance on a later occasion.

FURTHER VISITS FROM A LOVING SOUL

In this account our narrator gives us a convincing picture of the vitality a soul can possess after its transition. The story demonstrates the survival of love, and it shows the very real and positive effects that assurances of this enduring affection often have on the living.

"I had felt my first meeting with Artie would turn out to be an isolated happening, a one-time event, and would never be repeated. But the next summer, when I

went back to our hometown to help my relatives cele-
brate my mother-in-law's eighty-ninth birthday, I found
out I had been mistaken.

"The family was all together, having just sat down
in a cafeteria, when I looked up and there was Artie,
carrying a tray and coming toward us. He had on a white
sport shirt and navy trousers, just what he usually would
have worn. And it was so natural that he would want to
be there.

"I wanted to say, 'Look, Artie's here, too.' But this
was such a fleeting experience, lasting only for a second,
that I didn't mention it to anyone. Also, I didn't know
how the family would react, so I kept silent—though I
myself treasured the event. About a year later, when I
was visiting these relatives again, I did tell them about
Artie's two appearances to date, and they found them
quite interesting.

"My third visit from Artie was another very brief
one. It happened after the death of a dear seven-year-
old granddaughter, Sarah, as a result of a tragic accident.
I told her mother, my daughter, that Grandpa was taking
care of her, and she agreed that he would be.

"So I guess I wasn't really surprised one day to look
up and see Artie and Sarah standing there together, holding hands and smiling. Telepathically he was saying to
me, 'Yes, I have Sarah, and I am looking after her.'

"Artie's fourth appearance was a real shocker. Because it came four years later, the impact of losing him
had lessened, and I was growing accustomed to the separation. This experience was very real and lasted much
longer than the others.

"At the time, I belonged to a Jewish-Christian inter-
faith group that was presenting a lecture by a distin-
guished speaker. The group gave a dinner party before
the address so that we could meet the speaker and talk
with him, and I was attending the get-together. It was
one of the few times I had been at such a gathering since
my husband's death, at least among people with whom

I was not really close friends. Most of the people there were couples, so I was probably the only single person present.

"Before the dinner began I was sitting on a couch with a couple of women I had just met and with whom I had been talking. I had turned away, feeling alone and very lonely, when I looked up toward a picture window across the room, and there stood Artie! He was perfectly relaxed and at ease, with a great big smile on his face and one hand in a pocket of the beautiful blue suit he usually wore to socials.

"He looked so wonderful, so bright. I don't mean in a light-up sort of way, but just so full of life and energy that he was almost shining with an inner glow—and so young! I know that this is a funny thing to say about someone who has died, but it is true.

"And again, he had a silent message for me: 'Yes, I know it's tough, I know it's hard, but I'm not really that far away from you.' Such a simple message, yet so wonderful.

"The vision, or whatever it was, had several overtones. There was an implied approval of the activity in which I was participating. Somehow I also felt a farewell, as though Artie wanted me to know he was going on to something else, and this was good-bye. I was filled with such a sense of peace and exhilaration that I'm not too sure what happened the rest of the evening. This feeling lasted for several weeks.

"I was downtown the week after the social, and there I met a man who used to work for my husband. I almost blurted out, 'Oh, Reggie, I saw Art last week and he looked so good!'—just as you would say about anyone who had been away for a while.

"I have no complete explanation for these happenings. I know that they were real and wonderful and that they reaffirmed my own beliefs. I also know I will never be afraid to die. I think that perhaps if there is a strong bond among people while they are alive, it's not unreasonable to suppose this bond is sometimes powerful enough to break through the barrier of death. Also, as someone pointed out to me, all four of Artie's appearances occurred at times when I was under stress; perhaps that had something to do with allowing these events to happen.

"I think it is not good for anyone to hold onto someone after death, to grieve so excessively and for such a long time that the deceased might feel earthbound by the sorrow and not be able to go on with his or her development. I certainly had not done this with Artie.

"I will always be extremely grateful for these experiences, and I wish I could share them more. I've told very few people about them, and only people who I know will accept them as valid—those who won't react like one woman, who said, 'I don't want to think about people coming back from the dead'; or another who remarked, 'Oh, that's terrible. I wouldn't like that.' These people are entitled to their opinions, of course. But if you haven't had the experience, don't knock it." *M. A.*

Our next report is unusual in that it combines descriptions of one person's waking experience and another's dream. With both receiving the same message from the same source and at the same time, we have impressive evidence that communication with the dead truly did take place. The continued love of the deceased for the living is clearly depicted here, as is the beneficial effect of the reassurance they gave. Perhaps in this case it was the urgency of the husband's prayer that brought about the contact.

COMFORT FROM THE DECEASED

In life, we sometimes show our concern for our loved ones by stilling their fears and putting their minds at ease. With this story, my correspondent shows that the dead can express their devotion for us in the same way.

"My wife was in labor. She was having great difficulty and we feared for her life. I got down on my knees at her bedside and began to pray with all my heart, mind, and soul.

"Suddenly a bright light appeared in a corner of the room where my wife lay, and I saw my father and mother looking at me and smiling. My father spoke and said, 'Everything will be all right. Your wife will give birth to a baby boy.'

"At almost the same moment my wife awakened, smiled, and said, 'I just had a wonderful dream! Your mother and father were here, and they said that everything would be all right and that we would have a son.'

"And so it was." *H. C.*

The following story gives another vivid picture of the enduring affection between parent and child. It also brings out several of the ideas we met in the preceding chapter. The physical improvement of souls on the other side is shown, as is their continuing need to learn, to develop, and to gain experience.

VISITING WITH A BELOVED SON

This account was contributed by a woman who lost her son at a young age. But, as can easily be seen here, she never lost his love.

"I will attempt to relate my dreams to you, as I feel I was communicating with my son, who died in January 1980 at the age of nine. My son's death was due to cancer and was not unexpected when it occurred. At the end we had not been able to say good-bye, though I did speak to him while he was unconscious.

"In September 1980 I dreamed that I saw him. He was in a classroom setting and working in the far corner of the room from me. I could not get near him. I was stopped by a presence if I tried to approach my son or communicate with him. I was told just to observe.

"My boy appeared the same physically as he had in life, though he was walking without difficulty. Prior to his death he had been paralyzed from the waist down, but he had finally managed to get around with a very stiff and awkward gait. This problem was not present in the dream.

"My next contact with my son occurred in August of 1982. In a dream, he was physically sitting at a table, and I was allowed to sit there with him. We were not permitted to speak, but I could hold his hand. His appearance was approximately as I remembered him, except that his eyelids were fluttering.

"At one point I said something about his eyes being unusual, and he began to fade. I realized then that he had been trying to maintain his bodily form for my reassurance and that what I had seen was not his normal state.

"In July 1985 I dreamed that my son was alive. He simply appeared and stayed with us a few days. It felt so good just to hug him! He and his brother played together as if they were both alive and both the same size. I even wondered about plans for school and what I would tell people after he left. We did not discuss the death process or where he had been.

"After a time he began to fade and to collapse. He said that he realized he must leave again, adding that it was what he needed and we were not to worry. He told me he loved me and said good-bye. He hugged and kissed me, and then he was physically gone." *P. H.*

OUR ATTITUDES AND BELIEFS
LIVE ON

I mentioned in an earlier chapter that the passing of the body can offer us a new perspective of the continuing life of the soul. This might lead some of us to expect that at death our entire mental make-up will be changed drastically and instantaneously. We might anticipate that in the afterlife everyone will be different, wiser.

Tempting as such an idea may be, it overlooks each soul's continuing existence as a free-willed individual. Death does not make one person into someone else; it does not automatically change attitudes and beliefs. This principle was demonstrated to me by a woman who needed encouragement to free herself from a restrictive mental pattern of her deceased husband. She seemed to have forgotten that he was still the same man he had been before he died.

This woman asked me about her experiences with her late husband. After he had been dead for five years or more, she met another man whom she came to love and who wanted to marry her. She hesitated because her departed husband appeared to her, pointed at a picture of her new friend, frowned, and shook his head. She interpreted this as implying that her contemplated marriage would not be a good one, so she refused to see the man any more. A few years later she met and grew fond of someone else who wanted to marry her. But again her husband appeared and expressed his disapproval.

It was at this point that she told me her story. I asked her, "Was your deceased husband jealous?"

"Oh!" she said. "It nearly ruined our marriage."

I recognized the problem instantly and told her, "I have news for you—he hasn't changed! Tell him you're lonely, you love this man, and you will marry him."

This the woman did, and she is now very happily married. Her departed husband has moved on.

In a similar way, I met another woman whose departed husband retained attitudes he had had before passing on. Here, the man continued to value an object that had been especially important to him in life. The widow experienced a series of visits soon after she remarried. In a conversation about her troubling experiences, she asked me, "Why does my dead husband keep appearing, pointing to my wedding ring, and shaking his head?"

I inquired if there was anything unusual about the ring. She said, "Nothing that I know of."

Then I asked if perchance the ring was an heirloom handed down through her family or perhaps her former husband's. She told me that she had lost the ring given her by her new spouse, and the present ring was the one her deceased husband had given her.

Now I understood. Of course, her former husband did not want her to wear his ring when married to another man! I suggested that she have her current husband buy her another ring and thus permit her ex-spouse to go on in peace. She followed this advice, and the disquieting visits ceased. I am sure her first husband was more content also.

Our religious and philosophical beliefs are another part of us that is likely to remain consistent after our transition. Edgar Cayce made this point in a humorous but instructive way. In one reading, he said that at death enlightenment does not automatically follow because of an individual's membership in a particular religious denomination. Rather, there is great potential benefit to be derived from *any* system of belief that points us toward a single ideal based upon the love of God. Furthermore, we carry that religious point of view with us into the afterlife. As Cayce put it: "... do not consider for a moment ... that an individual soul-entity passing from an earth plane as a Catholic, a Methodist, an Episcopalian, is something else because he is dead! He's only a dead Episcopalian, Catholic or Methodist.''   (254-92)

The continuity of belief is shown in the story of a man I knew in Houston. His thought system in this life affected his experiences in the next. He found what he *expected* to find following the transition. Like the story of the drowning ghost (whom we met in the preceding chapter), death did not cause him to immediately transcend his bias against reincarnation. Unfortunately his wife gave too much credence to the statements she heard in an after-death contact.

The story begins with our Cayce study group that had been meeting in their home during the period when the husband was dying of cancer. This man felt that reincarnation and many of the other concepts the group discussed were untrue. He believed that we have one life only, during which we create our destiny for eternity. One evening, shortly after the group had met, the man died.

A brief time thereafter, his wife reported that he had appeared to her in a dream state and said, ''I told you—there is no such thing as reincarnation.'' So the woman ceased her activity with the study group.

There are many people who believe that when a soul passes on it suddenly becomes ''all-wise.'' Fortunately or unfortunately, this is not true—hence the need for many incarnations. The beliefs and disbeliefs an individual holds during this lifetime will continue after death, and that soul will probably come into its next experience in physical life with this same view of spiritual matters. We do not go to heaven; we must grow to it!

CONTINUED ACHIEVEMENT ON THE OTHER SIDE

Our existence after death is but the next phase of life. Just as we who are still physically alive have goals to reach, those who have passed on continue to have the opportunity for positive accomplishments. There is work to be done, even on the other side. As several of my reports show, in some cases the deceased will remain engaged in activities similar to those the person had performed before crossing over. Evidently, at least some of the means of service and growth open to souls beyond death are not too different from those available to us in physical life.

This point was illustrated in a number of Edgar Cayce's dreams, in which he saw the creation of a place in the afterlife where he could continue to give psychic readings once he had moved into that dimension. In one example Mr. Cayce's dream showed that the need to use the special talents he had developed during his life would not end with his death. The dream brought out one of the most hopeful implications of reincarnation: The abilities that we strive to gain during physical life will not pass away when we leave the body behind. They remain a part of us, and they will be ours to draw upon in the future. Mr. Cayce reported his dream as follows:

''I found myself in the nether land, and I recognized the place as being along the route I had traveled in going to the 'House of Records' to secure past-life information for the life readings. Many people I knew were there. I told them we had to build a place there where we could give readings, as we did on the earth. I then met a man whom I recognized as a builder and asked him to construct the house for me.

"At first the man said, 'I have my own house. Why should I have to work here?'

"I answered, 'As in the earth we worked, so must we work here also. If we are satisfied and just sit down here, we'll never get up yonder and find Him whom we are seeking. He, Jesus, may pass this way, but we won't be ready to go anywhere unless we are doing something. I think we've got a lot to tell these people.

" 'It's beautiful, it's lovely, and it's quiet here. We don't have to worry about wind, or weather, or something to eat, or night and day, or anything else, because it's whatever we want. But remember, He told us we must always do everything in decency and order.'

"So the builder said, 'I know some of the other fellows here—O.K., we'll build it.' " (294-196 Supplement)

One might say this is an interesting dream but still wonder if there is any truth to it. Did Edgar Cayce actually continue to give people helpful guidance after his death? From my own personal experience, I can answer a definite *Yes*.

EDGAR CAYCE STILL ON CALL

The following incident showed me beyond a doubt that Cayce is still using his talent and that he continues to be concerned with easing the physical ailments of others, just as he had been during his earthly lifetime.

Some years ago I developed an allergy to seafood. Since I eat no pork and very little beef, foods such as fish have been an important part of my diet. So I prayed one night asking if there was something I could do to allow me to eat seafood. I then had a vision in which I saw an outstretched hand holding some garlic. When I tried the remedy suggested in this vision, I found that

I could eat seafood with impunity if I followed the meal with a hefty capsule of garlic oil.

One night, after eating fish and taking the garlic oil, I broke out in hives! For three days and nights I was in agony. So I prayed again, "Why, O Lord, why?" This time I saw a picture of two horses pulling a carriage, immediately followed by a scene of four horses pulling another carriage. To me, the message was clear: double the strength of the garlic pill.

But to be sure, I went into meditation with the question, "Have I made the right interpretation?" In answer, I heard the voice of Edgar Cayce say one word—"Exactly!" It seemed to come from miles away in space. Need I say, the remedy worked. Cayce was still available to help me. There is no death of the soul!

The same continuity of activity is described in another story about contact with the deceased—in this case, with Edgar Cayce's son, Hugh Lynn. Here we can see Hugh Lynn making constructive use of his personal talents and carrying on the same type of work that he had been involved in before his death. He continues to show the same interest in people and to serve them in the same way as he had during physical life.

COUNSELING CONTINUES

This account conveys a sense of the deep personal bond between our narrator and his deceased advisor. It also gives us a vivid picture of the happiness a soul can find after death and how that joy can be enhanced by keeping busy in positive ways.

"While I was in the navy, I used to go to Virginia Beach once a week to see Hugh Lynn Cayce for private counseling sessions. I continued in this practice until he passed on in July of 1982. He helped me in more ways than I can say here, and after his departure I wondered if he ever knew how great a benefit I had derived from my contact with him.

"About six months after Hugh Lynn's passing, I had a dream in which I was in a place that seemed to be a 'vibratory office'—it looked like an office, but was more colorful, bright, and ethereal. When I walked in, I sensed (rather than saw) a lot of people sitting in a waiting room. I was holding a box or present in my hand.

"Hugh Lynn came out into the waiting room, and I gave him the present. I don't know what was in the box, but he seemed pleased and thanked me for it. He looked very 'bright,' as I remembered him. He seemed especially happy and busy. I realized that he was carrying on the counseling work that he had done in the earth, but now he was counseling souls at a higher level.

"After I awoke, I sensed that he now knew of my gratitude for the help he had given me during his lifetime."   *R. G.*

GROWTH AND DEVELOPMENT IN THE AFTERLIFE

As many of our stories have shown, after death the soul tends to retain the personality traits, emotional attachments, attitudes, beliefs, and talents it possessed in materiality. It can even continue on in the same work it had done before the transition. But this continuity does not mean that at death our existence becomes static. Change is possible on the other side.

This is a very hopeful idea since virtually all of us pass from this life with personal difficulties still unresolved. Death does not eliminate all our problems or make us over into new people. It also does not end our opportunity *to work on* those problems. The deceased can continue to grow, to learn, and—if need be—to improve themselves and their relationships with others.

Each of these points can be seen in our next two stories, which were sent to me by the same person.

RECONCILIATION AFTER DEATH

This report shows that the difficult relationship between my correspondent and her mother was not instantaneously smoothed over by the mother's death. But the possibility of working on the problems and improving the association continued even after her demise.

"The majority of my contacts have been with my mother, and most of these—though not all—have occurred in dreams.

"While my mother was alive and very much a force in my life, I began having dreams in which she shouted at me and berated me. At that time I couldn't see that, in fact, she was dominating me in unhealthy ways.

"Although her death in 1973 from a car accident was a terrible shock to me, it also brought me a sense of being released—freed. Only now am I coming to appreciate how much I needed that release. Even with it, I'm having a struggle to get free of her influence. Now my dreams of my mother almost always involve my lecturing to her—discussing what her effect on me used to be and standing up for my own choices and my own point of view.

"This past spring, while reading David Spangler's *Revelation* and M. Scott Peck's *The Road Less Traveled*, I was shown that when I was a teen-ager my parents sold my only friend—a horse! I made this discovery in a dream in which I was angry with my parents for selling the horse. In that dream my father was driving our car. I was in the passenger seat, and my mother was in back. I turned to her at one point and said ominously, 'Well, you're running up quite a tab, aren't you?'

"At first I assumed the dream was not literally about

the sale of the horse, but all day I felt weird about it and threatened, as though something dreadful was about to get me. Finally it emerged. It was the realization that I was angry, had mistrusted and hated my parents for selling the horse, and had never forgiven them for doing so.

"After dealing with these emotions for a while, I decided to see if Mom was present. I spoke to her and felt that she was there. She seemed to be asking what she could do to have me forgive her. At first I said there was nothing; the damage had been done.

"But then I realized that I also was feeling guilty about the horse—I had been dreaming about her for years and years. I asked, 'How's my horse? Are they taking care of her?' I told my mother that the only thing she could do was to find the horse, even if my former pet had already been reborn. I held my mother responsible for the animal's well-being. I wanted her to bring the horse to me or show me that she was O.K. and hadn't suffered.

"When I said this, my mother seemed to be relieved, as though glad to have something that she could do for me."   *P. C.*

ENCOURAGEMENT FROM THE DECEASED

As with the relationship to her mother, our contributor had also remaining issues with her father—problems that were not eliminated by his passing. Quite possibly, the sincere desire for reconciliation on the part of all three of them is helping to bring about the ongoing healing evident in these two accounts.

"My most significant experience with my deceased father came this past March. I had a dream about starting a Ph.D. program in English at the University of Denver, as I had once wanted to do. Both parents appeared in the dream, and my mother made some carping remarks. But my father insisted that I should enter the program and said emphatically that he would pay for it.

"I awakened then and sensed his presence, for only the second time since his death. We were able to communicate with each other and to clear up some issues left between us. This was not too hard because, although he had been distant and lukewarm in life, he had never actually lied to me or tried to control me. I felt that he meant what he had said about the Ph.D. I came away thinking that maybe I did want the degree and that somehow he had pledged himself to providing me with the needed funds. I don't know how or when he will fulfill this promise, but I accept it and I trust him.

"In my experiences so far in communicating with the deceased, I have learned that I can talk to a discarnate person and get a response. This is true whether the contact occurs in a dream or while I am awake. I've also noticed that those who come to me seem to follow certain rules. The chief rule: if they can't say something helpful, they're not to say anything at all. This is good for me because I've always had a rough time being listened to by any authority figure. It is lovely to be able to speak my mind without being attacked as a result.

"Somebody—whoever is in charge of this interaction—is protecting me from psychic attack and providing only open opportunities to learn, grow, and communicate. I'm very grateful for this because, though by nature I am an explorer and willing to take risks, I have been made timid in some ways by my background. But after five-and-one-half years of this interaction among the planes, I feel quite comfortable experimenting with it.

"Probably my biggest surprise about all this is how much my mother and I still have to clear up between us. Each time she visits I tell her what's on my mind, answer what seems to be her question, and feel that we're making great strides. Then a week or two later I find I'm still having to defend myself, fight with her, and be involved in arguments we never had while she was alive!

"Absolutely the most encouraging thing I've sensed is that after people leave the earth they go on learning about the life they've just finished living. Relationships can improve, people can keep growing in wisdom, and families can continue to evolve." *P. C.*

Our final story of this chapter is one of my favorites. Here we meet a soul who continues to be involved in the same type of work as before he crossed over. He also retains a personal habit that he had had during physical life, and the discovery of this habit, previously unknown to my correspondent, lends a great deal of credibility to this report.

But this account is primarily concerned with the significant changes in personality an individual can undergo following the transition. It gives us a very encouraging picture of human potential for growth and improvement after death, even in cases where that potential may not have been apparent during physical life. There is a strong implication here that the prayers of the living can play an important role in helping the deceased make constructive use of their ability to change.

DOUG, THE HUMMER, FINDS HEAVEN

The contributor of this story used prayer to build a bridge between himself and a hard-to-reach associate. Through his efforts came joy and success where there had been bitter failure, and genuine friendship where before there had been isolation. These results offer us the uplifting message that our actions on behalf of others can bring forth beautiful fruits, even after death.

"Doug was a business associate. He was a loner, hard to get along with, creative, detail-oriented, impractical, and an alcoholic. I didn't especially like him. Doug had had a very difficult life which included a period as a prisoner of war in a Japanese camp during World War II. Later he suffered a series of business failures, always after he had been involved in successful enterprises. He seemed to lose everything on long-shot ventures. When he drank, he became belligerent and obnoxious, and no one wanted to be around him.

"In time, Doug developed a liver disease which eventually took his life. I visited him in the hospital before he died, and I prayed for him until he passed on. For eleven months after his demise, I continued to pray for him; since he had never been very well-liked, I felt that not too many people would be doing so.

"One night Doug visited me in a dream, and he looked wonderful! He appeared to be healthy, happy, and enthusiastic. He told me he was grateful to me. I assumed he was referring to my prayers, so I didn't ask him why. I told him how marvelous he looked and what a fantastic adjustment he had made to losing his family—a wife and son—the year before. (In the dream, I had the feeling that they had died, and Doug and I were alive.)

"Doug wanted me to see where he worked, and because he was so excited I went with him. We entered a nicely furnished office, and he introduced me to a man I took to be his partner. Doug was humming the entire time. I was amazed that even when he took a telephone call he managed to talk and hum simultaneously, without letting one interfere with the other. He was obviously a success finally, and I was genuinely pleased for him. He showed me an empty desk and told me I could have an equal share of the business if I wished. I thanked him but told him I couldn't accept, because I had other commitments.

"The day after having this dream I called Bart, a friend of Doug's who had looked after him frequently while he was alive, and told him of my experience. Bart laughed and laughed and said that not many people knew of Doug's passion for humming. He did it only when he thought no one was around, but Bart had heard it many times. He was pleased and thanked me for the good news. I never heard from Doug again."

H. G.

What is especially noteworthy about this final story is a theme we have observed throughout this chapter: continuity *and* change. Elements of the personality carry over, but the opportunity to change and grow is also there. What a comforting thought! The transition called death need not cause us to be afraid since we will still know ourselves in the familiar way. At the same time, the new life into which we are born opens up additional chances for soul development.

7

REASSURANCE FROM THE DEAD

WHEN A FRIEND or loved one dies, perhaps what we, who are left behind, want more than anything else is reassurance. We desire some sign or event that will convince us that everything is all right for the one who has passed on. We should not feel guilty for such a desire—it is a natural part of being human. It does not mean that our faith in God has failed or that our belief in the afterlife is shaky. We want reassurance simply because we care so much for that individual. The accounts that have been sent to me convincingly show that the deceased are often willing and able to provide that assurance.

COMFORT FROM DEPARTED FRIENDS

In this first story our narrator tells of two departed friends who returned to bring her messages of consolation. These visits demonstrate the concern the dead can feel for the living, and the very real and positive effects their expression of this concern can have.

"A close friend, who was in her seventies, was very unhappy about her circumstances, particularly conditions involving her marriage. She felt she had not received the security she thought she should have. She began to feel ill, and after several days she dropped dead unexpectedly.

"Several months after her death, I sensed that she was sitting in a chair by the table in my kitchen. She had a sweet smile on her face and appeared beautifully relaxed. We seemed to converse telepathically. She communicated only two words: 'It's beautiful.' I felt she meant that she was in a beautiful place. The impression then faded, and I was left with the definite feeling that she had really spoken to me, letting me know she was happy.

"Approximately a year later, a young friend died unexpectedly in his sleep. This man was only in his twenties. He had grown up with my son, and I felt as badly about his passing as if he were one of my own. I cried every time I thought of him.

"One morning while preparing breakfast, and sobbing, I heard his voice saying, 'Don't cry, Mrs. L.'

"I answered aloud, 'I won't.' This message comforted me, as I felt it had come directly from him."

B. L.

Both incidents related in this report illustrate a reassuring theme that is quite common in the material I have received: The dead generally have a pleasant existence on the other side, and they really don't need us to grieve for them. This is true even in cases where the person had been discontented in material life, as in the first episode; and in ones where the death appears to be untimely, as in the second.

Many accounts also reveal that the departed are still aware of our feelings and still care about us. It frequently seems that their love is what prompts them to contact us; they want to offer us the consolation that can be found in knowing that life continues, often joyfully. That the dead live on is the most basic message they communicate in their contacts with the living—and perhaps the most comforting. The next story gives us a simple, direct affirmation of this fundamental truth.

A BLISSFUL END TO SEPARATION

In the first incident described here, my correspondent is shown that the separation caused by death is not permanent. The second episode demonstrates that the deceased can perceive, appreciate, and return our expressions of love for them. Together, these messages give us quite a reassuring picture of existence on the other side of life.

"Shortly after my father died I went into light meditation in order to see where he was. Instantly I found myself at the beach. There stood my father, and with him was my mother, who had passed on long before. Separated in life, they were brought together in death.

"Yes, we do live on. I know that! Last March my brother died. A month or so later my sister phoned me, upset over some unkind things someone had said about him. I was sure these reports about my brother were untrue, and I defended him. After I had hung up the phone I turned out the light, ready to go to sleep. Instantly my right foot was squeezed, as in a friendly handshake. I knew my brother was present and had heard the conversation.

"Interestingly, I was recovering from a broken foot at the time, and it was the good foot that was squeezed. He had known which one to touch. Yes, there is life after death!"   *C. W. B.*

The following report also involves a message of reassurance that was received in waking life. Here we see that the dead are alive and that they can remain close to us and can be responsive. The soul we meet in this story has an interesting and surprising way to get this comforting message across.

REASSURANCE FROM A BELOVED FATHER

I found two features of this account most moving: our contributor's great need for consolation at the time the incident took place and the remarkable ability of a departed soul to fill that need.

"I once had an experience that really shook me up. I am Armenian, and one Sunday morning I had been listening to an Armenian radio program. The songs they were playing brought back a lot of memories of ones my dead father used to sing. When the program was over, I turned off the radio, and I really missed my father terribly, for we had been very close. I started to cry. Finally I said out loud, 'Dad, if you can hear what I'm saying to you, please give a sign so I'll know you're here with me.' Then I went about my work.

"A few hours later, while I was in the kitchen, where the radio was, it suddenly came on by itself! Now in all the years I've had a radio this has never happened before, and I know I definitely had turned that radio off. I was thrilled by this occurrence because, to me, it was a sign that my dear father had heard me and was there with me."   *C. R.*

Like the preceding story, our next report tells of a parent's reassuring message that death has not ended his existence. In this account my correspondent vividly describes the great joy the encounter brings to her. We can also see here the survival of personality, as shown in the departed soul's continuing to attend services and to be unconcerned about matters of dress.

A FATHER STILL ATTENDS CHURCH SERVICES

In this story our narrator gives us a joyful picture of a loving parent-child relationship that endures even beyond the grave. This relationship was featured in the concluding story to Chapter 5.

"My first unusual dream involving Daddy occurred about six months after his death. In the dream, I was in my home church, sitting in the middle of a crowded pew. There were more people in the church than I remember ever having seen. Our minister was conducting the services. I looked up and saw my father, sitting in the minister's chair behind him.

"As soon as I became aware of Daddy, he got up, walked slowly down to the end of the pew where I was sitting, stopped, and smiled at me. I made my way out of the pew, and a feeling of intense joy ran through me. I threw my arms around him and said, over and over again, 'You're real! You're real! You're real!'

"He did not speak, but somehow I perceived an answer of 'Yea' from him. I awoke, shaking and crying with joy.

"Then I started to laugh, because Daddy had been dressed in one of his 'everything matches' golfing outfits, and it was wrinkled beyond all imagination. He could not have chosen a better symbol to get across to me his unconcern about neatness, even in this, his new life."

B. L. D.

Our next story, which comes from the same source as the previous one, shows again the close relationship between father and daughter and the reassurance of his continued existence. In addition, it offers a comforting thought: the truth can encompass all belief systems. There is the suggestion that my respondent's father knew of her difficulty with her church and that it was his loving desire to help her with this problem which prompted him to deliver this message to her. The account closes with a statement of the helpful impact of his visit.

AN IMPORTANT REVELATION

At the time of the dream related here, our contributor had been having doubts regarding the formal aspects of her devotional life. Her father's appearance demonstrated that those who have passed on can still be there for us with needed advice and guidance. This thought can be a comforting and reassuring one to any of us.

"My second dream about my dead father started with the two of us in a setting which I thought, at the time, to be something like a world's fair. We were going to exhibitions and watching people on rides. After a while, I became aware that I wanted to go and see the live presentation of the painting, *The Last Supper*.

"It became an obsession with me to get to this showing. Daddy and I seemed to be delayed many times, and my expectations grew. Finally, we had to crawl through a dirt hole to reach the large cave where the exhibition was being staged.

"When at last we arrived, many people were there. Some were kneeling in front of the table, others at random throughout the large room. Everyone was either praying or looking with awe at the presentation. I was on my knees, and I slowly looked up to the stage, expecting something of great beauty and inspiration.

"I was stunned with disbelief! In the first place, the actors had on too much make-up. Their robes were ragged and dull, and they seemed to be bored with the entire experience. I was both amazed and distressed at what I saw.

"I looked again at the others around me, and I couldn't understand why everyone was unable to see how fake and awful the presentation was. I thought to myself that there must be something wrong with my understanding—how could I be all alone in seeing things so negatively?

"I looked at Daddy, who looked back at me, and I became aware that he was in pain. His pain and discomfort grew more and more apparent, and I became agitated as well as worried.

"My brother and my father's brother suddenly appeared, one on each side of Daddy. My brother seemed to be older than he was at that time, and my uncle appeared younger than he actually was. They looked to be about the same age, and their faces were glowing. They had expressions of great peace and radiated health and well-being. They reached out and took hold of my father, and immediately he, too, was at peace. The three of them then all smiled at me, turned, and walked away.

"When I woke up, I had no trouble interpreting the Last Supper portion of the dream. It seemed reasonable to equate my conscious feelings of being out of step with my church with the way I had felt standing alone in front of what I perceived to be a gross misrepresentation of something holy, while everyone else was struck with awe.

"I wrestled for several days with the second part of the dream. It haunted me. I knew the meaning was what I needed, but it wouldn't surface. When I finally saw the light, it was blinding!

"My brother, who is my father's only son, was heavily into the Eastern religions. When I had last been home, we had talked many hours about reincarnation and the implications of that concept. My father's brother was part of the born-again Christian movement and actively preached against astrology and psychic events of any kind. So in these two people all the elements of my struggle in relation to my church were represented.

"To me, this part of the dream conveyed a message from my father that said, 'Don't despair. The answer will encompass us all!' This idea was a great comfort to me. It allowed me to go on searching for my version of 'Truth' and gave me faith that I could not fence myself off from God or salvation."

B. L. D.

VISITS FROM A JOYOUS SOUL

One reassuring concept appears again and again in the material I have received: the dead enjoy a *happy state of existence* on the other side of life. This can be seen in our next story, which gives us a picture of a continuing good-natured relationship between my correspondent and a deceased friend. The report is notable for its relaxed, joyful tone and for the complete naturalness of the soul's presence in our narrator's dreams. The portrait our contributor paints here is of a delightfully, infectiously happy soul, whose consistent good spirits would be hard to rival in this world or the next.

"My deceased friend has been present in several of my dreams. In one, he and I are in a large gymnasium with about twenty other people. He is happy and healthy; yet in the dream I know he is dead. He is teaching me what it's like to be out of the body. Quite suddenly I realize that I am flying around the ceiling while our bodies are still on the floor. It is exhilarating.

"In another dream my friend is on the phone. His voice sounds distant, and he is saying that it is O.K. about M. G., an associate of his who committed suicide.

"Whenever my friend appears in a dream, he is a merry kind of presence—he's just sort of 'around,' though the dream may not seem to be about him. My feeling is 'Oh, there is my friend.' But simultaneously I know that he has moved on. Therefore, I've often felt that he is indeed present and that our relationship has continued, and not that he is simply a dream symbol in the usual sense."   *L. C.*

One element of this report might seem surprising: the idea that even a person who has taken his or her own life can be all right in the next world. This same feature may be present in our next account, which possibly involves contact with a suicide. However the woman in this story died, the important point is her repeated assurance that she is O.K. and that worry about her is unnecessary.

A SOUL IS "HOME" AND HAPPY

I received this report from a person who was evidently feeling some uneasiness over the possibility that an acquaintance had killed herself. The soul's visit, conveying the message that she was all right, must have taken a great burden off our narrator's mind.

"One of my experiences was with a woman named Ann, whom I had known for only a year. We had never been close friends, but we associated with the same people and often met in various places. During several of these meetings, we had had deep discussions about faith.

"One night, as a result of an explosion and fire in her apartment, Ann died. Those who knew her were evenly divided in their opinions as to whether her death was accidental or a suicide. At the time, I was firmly convinced it had been an accident.

"I didn't find out where or when Ann's funeral was held until two days after the service, and that made me very angry. I had wanted to say good-bye to someone I considered a good person, and to be denied the opportunity to do so made me see red!

"About three weeks after Ann died, I was washing dishes and thinking of her. Suddenly I heard her voice saying, 'I'm O.K.' In my mind I expressed my sorrow at missing her funeral. She said, 'Don't worry about it. I'm O.K.'

"Then, mentally, I asked her, 'Was it an accident or not?'

"Her answer was, 'I'm where I want to be. I'm O.K. Don't worry about me. I'm happy.' And abruptly she was out of my presence as fast as she'd entered. I believed her and quit worrying.

"The following year I met someone who had been living across the street from Ann when she died. He told me how he had stood on the sidewalk and watched the firemen put out the blaze. One of the firemen, who had been inside the apartment, had said to him that Ann's body looked as though she had knelt down and stuck her head in the gas oven. The firemen were sure it was suicide; but, since no insurance or other legal problem was involved, they had called it an accident to spare the family's feelings."   *K. B.*

Our next story describes a transformation of fear to happiness and illustrates how that happiness can be communicated to the living. An interesting sidelight to this report is my correspondent's reluctance to return to normal waking life. This is a feature we will see again in a later chapter of out-of-body and near-death experiences. This resistance to returning may be another indication of the joy to be found in the realm our narrator experienced with his departed friend.

VISITS FROM A MERRY, MISCHIEVOUS SPIRIT

The contributor of this account tells us of two meetings with a very appealing ghost. The story vividly shows that death neither takes away this soul's personal characteristics nor disrupts her ability to enjoy life.

"Anna was a special woman. She was a free-lance writer and a world traveler. She had psychic gifts and had done some volunteer work at the library of the A.R.E. in Virginia Beach.

"Anna had chronic emphysema. She came back to Hawaii to spend her final months. Shortly before she was admitted to the Hospice at Saint Frances, I met her for the first time, through a friend. About a month later she wrote and asked to be placed on our prayer list for healing.

"At this time another friend suggested we visit Anna at the hospice. We brought her some fruit and stayed to pray and meditate with her. She asked me to aid her in her transition, and I said that I would.

"Anna lived for two years or more after our first visit, physically deteriorating throughout the period. I went to see her several times a week and prayed for her daily. At times she was very frightened and asked me to stay with her. I spent a number of nights sleeping in a chair in her room. In time, she passed on.

"Two months after Anna's death she came to visit me in a dream. She was young and pretty, and she wore a beautiful peach-colored dress of satin and lace. I was very happy to see her so healthy and beautifully dressed! We walked across a lawn and she told me how good she felt.

"Later in that dream I found myself sitting in an empty hospital room with her. A man who had just had surgery was brought in, which surprised us, since we had thought we had the room to ourselves. Then an orderly came into the room with a food cart. Even though he could neither see nor hear us, Anna had somehow called him in. He became confused when he realized what he had done, for no apparent reason. Anna was delighted with her prank and the man's confusion. She and I both laughed at her mischievous deed.

"About a month later, Anna came to me in another dream. She was with a male friend. We prepared some food together, and she told me she was going away. I asked her to stay, but she said they both had to go. I asked if I could accompany them. She said, 'No, it would not be possible.' I didn't know where they were going. I knew only that I wanted to go with them."

H. G.

WELL-BEING IN THE AFTERLIFE

Many people would say that good health is an important ingredient of happiness during physical life. The situation doesn't seem to change too much with death, even though the body a soul has in the afterlife is not quite the same as a flesh body. The deceased often seem to enjoy a healthy condition. In fact, it may seem a bit odd to speak of the dead being in good health. But I have received a number of reports of visits from individuals who, like Anna, had been persistently ill in life, and yet they became models of vitality after their transition. Such stories convey the heartening message that any sickness—even one that takes a person's physical life—can be overcome. This reassurance, one of the most powerful the dead can offer us, is to be found in both of our next accounts.

A HAPPY, HEALTHY GHOST

This story clearly shows the connection between health and happiness on the other side. Quite probably, the desire of my correspondent's friend to display her renewed vigor was important in prompting her to pay her first visit.

*   *   *

"I had a dream in which a deceased friend kept running through my apartment. She was clothed in a white dress trimmed in orange. Her shoes and purse matched the orange trim on the dress. I thought it was lovely! She appeared full of joy and good health. She had been very ill before her death, and I understood that she wanted me to know that she was now well and happy.

"In a later dream she appeared to me and said, 'This is the last time I will be able to come.' We then sat down in a restaurant and talked. I do not remember what was said, but I felt it was important. True to her initial statement, I have not seen her again."   *A. F.*

A PICTURE OF RESTORED HEALTH

Here we meet another soul who has passed from a condition of physical illness to one of vibrant well-being in the afterlife. The joyful reassurance this transformation brings, to both the departed and our narrator, is unmistakable.

"Leo was a member of our A.R.E. study group in Davenport, Iowa. Periodically he had to be hospitalized. One day my wife and I stopped off to visit Leo on our way home. We walked into his room about three minutes after he had died!

"Nearly a year later I had a vivid dream in which I was attending an A.R.E. meeting with a group of Association members whom I didn't know. We were meeting in the conference room of a motel. I was talking to someone when the door opened, and I saw my friend Leo standing there, grinning from ear to ear. He was the picture of health and was well dressed.

"I said, 'Leo, where have you been? I've been waiting for you.' We embraced, and the meeting started. Then I awakened."   *W. W.*

*   *   *

Our next account is in two parts. The first acknowledges
that the world may forget who we are after we have
passed away. But the second affirms that, even though
we may be forgotten, we will continue to live and that
in the next world our health can be regained.

ANSWERS TO TWO SOUL-SEARCHING QUESTIONS

The contributor of this story was obviously deeply affected by the death of a dear parent. There is, however,
an offer of hope for all of us in the account's closing
statement of the restoration of vitality in the afterlife.

"Using deep meditation, I asked two questions. First,
why did my mother's death go unnoticed by the world?
There were no newspaper headlines, no riderless horses,
no general mourning. She was as good as anyone who
will ever come this way, and yet her departure went
unnoticed. Why? Second, why had someone, as good as
she had been, died so horribly from the ravages of cancer and improper medical treatment?

"The answer to the first question was given me in a
vision of the deserts of Egypt. I was shown the Sphinx
and the great pyramids. A voice said, 'Tens of thousands
built these monuments to a handful of men. Millions
worshiped them as gods. Where are these men now?
Who were they? What did they think and care about?
Who cares about them today?' I saw the dust cover these
structures and I was told, 'It is the destiny of every man,
woman, and child to be forgotten. This is the nature of
humankind.'

"The answer to the second question came next. I saw
a black object that I could not identify. It pulled back,
and I could see two nostrils. As it withdrew farther I

could plainly see the dog we had had for thirteen years. She was not paralyzed as she had been in life, her coat was as golden as it had been when she was two or three years old, and she was strong and healthy. If I had been there physically, she would have jumped all over me.

"Then I saw my mother walk to the end of the table on which the dog was sitting and put her arm around her. My mother was wearing a beige dress with a belt. She looked young and healthy, showing no ravages from the chemotherapy she had endured.

"Someone said to me, 'We cannot explain to you why your mother underwent what she did; but we did not give your mother death. We gave her life.' " *B. Z.*

One of Edgar Cayce's own dream experiences shows that those whom we love are never lost. In Cayce's dream, he found himself in surroundings that led him to believe he might be in the spirit world—the land of the deceased. He wondered if he would be able to see his departed son, Milton Porter Cayce, who had died in infancy. The scene changed, and Mr. Cayce saw tiers and tiers of babies. Suddenly he recognized his own child. He realized that the child knew him as well, for he smiled at his father, but said nothing, and the dream ended.

In a subsequent psychic reading, a question was posed, asking for an interpretation of Cayce's dream. The response indicated that this had been an actual contact with his son and that this dream showed actual recognition between Cayce and his deceased baby boy.

His experience illustrates several themes that are present in some of the most moving reports I have received. These accounts make it clear that those who have died continue to recognize and love the people who had been close to them in life. They show that the expression of this continued recognition and affection, like Milton Porter Cayce's smile for his father, can bring great joy to the living. They also reassure us that the love two people feel for each other endures, even after one of them has passed on.

Both of these comforting truths are evident in our next two stories.

THE TOUCH OF A DEPARTED CHILD

In this simple story our narrator gives us an eloquent description of a soul's ability to respond to a loved one's need for consolation. This account confirms that our loving gestures have lasting effects, and the devotion they express can be returned, even from beyond death.

"Years ago I lost a small daughter quite suddenly. With my grief came a sense of guilt for the times I had been less than patient with her. On one occasion I had come home from work very tired. When she tried to climb into my lap I had forcefully said, 'Oh, don't. It's too hot!'

"This girl was actually the older of my two daughters. During the earlier part of her brief life, we had lived in an apartment. There the smaller one had slept in a crib, and at times the older girl had shared my bed. Sometimes I felt her stirring, and I would reach out and gently pat her hand to reassure her. When we moved from the apartment she began sharing a room with her younger sister, and I completely forgot about the hand-patting. After a time, she passed on.

"Soon after her demise, I had a dream which, though brief—dark and silent as the incidents it recalled—was clear and meaningful to me. My little girl came and patted my hand! I was truly comforted."   L. O.

A VISIT FROM A DEVOTED PARENT

A similar gesture of love is the subject of our next account. The experience of my correspondent's mother shows the continuing affection of the dead for the living and the enduring capacity of a mother's love to soothe her child's grief.

"My adoptive mother has had several remarkable experiences. One of them involved her mother, who died in 1984, at the age of ninety-three. Shortly after her passing, Gram 'popped' into my mother's room one night while she was awake and crying, sat on the edge of the bed, and gave her a hug! Mom says it was only after she got up the next morning that she remembered Gram had gone on. What a lovely thing to have happened!

"My mother cannot be fully sure, of course, that this experience was a vision; it might have been a dream. But under the circumstances—insomnia produced by extreme distress—it would seem that 'vision' is the best description."   *C. P. P.*

Our next story provides the same reassurance that love continues and a similar description of the powerful effect this message can have on the living. Along with the communication of affection, we are given a compelling picture of the joy a soul can experience after death.

A FATHER'S CONTENTMENT

Our contributor describes a combination of intense love and happiness. The story beautifully summarizes a central feature in most of the accounts in this chapter: In showing us their own happiness, the deceased are expressing their love for us by doing what they can to ease our grief and demonstrate that it is unwarranted.

"I would say that one of the most beautiful dreams I have ever had was about my father. It came to me approximately six months after he had died. In the dream I clearly saw him standing at a fence. I approached him and tried very hard to convince him to come home to my mother, who seemed to be living on the other side of the fence. He refused. Then he looked at me, and I saw the happiness in his face and eyes. I felt his great love and contentment.

"I awoke and realized, for the first time in six months, how much at peace and how happy and contented my father was where he had found himself. I also realized that he couldn't come back even if he wanted to. He left me with a love-filled feeling that was very wonderful.

"I have had other dreams about my father recently. He has been gone from this plane for five years now, and all of my experiences with him since his departure have emphasized how happy he is and how much love is there. He also tells me that he still loves me." *V. B.*

The closing story to this chapter on reassurance is one of the most hopeful I have received. It shows not only that love continues but that the capacity to express it can actually grow after death. Here our narrator gives us a clear description of her need to be reassured of her father's love. Though this need went unsatisfied during the man's lifetime, it was finally fulfilled after his passing. The report ends with the interesting suggestion that perhaps the dead can influence even the material world to reflect their love for us.

A FATHER AFFIRMS HIS LOVE

In this account our contributor shares with us a message that is both simple and profound: Death truly does not end our opportunity to express love for those dear to us.

"My father was fifty years old when I was born. I was his seventh child—the sixth girl. I always felt that he didn't want me, at least not another girl. He would rather have had a second boy.

"I can't remember my father ever saying he loved me. He would hold me on his knee at night and say, 'You're a good girl.' But I wanted more than that! I tried to please him in every way I could think of, from staying out of his way to doing everything I could for him.

"When I reached sixteen, I finally exploded and asked him very simply if he loved me. His response was, 'You're crazy.' After that I gave up and tried not to care, but for years this lack of assurance of his love caused me emotional problems, even after my marriage.

"The last time I saw my father before he died in 1976, he was suffering from cancer. I asked him again if he loved me. He turned his head away from me and said, 'I love all my children.' To me this seemed like another rejection, and I wept. A few years after my father's death, my brother also passed away. Some time later I had the following dream:

"My oldest sister and I were getting a meal ready in our old home. Our father and brother had come for a visit. They were sitting in the living room, and both appeared very serene, calm, and happy. As I walked past the recliner in which my father was leaning back, he reached out, caught my arm, and said, 'I love you.'

"After awakening I felt very strongly that my father had sent me this message. I believe that he is now aware of the unhappiness his inattention caused me, and that through this dream he was trying to let me know he had loved me in his way and still loves me.

"This last summer, the sister who had appeared in my dream gave me an old photographic slide that she had found, taken on her farm. It was of my father hugging me. It was incredible to me that I could have forgotten the incident, but I think that at the time it happened I didn't really believe it meant anything. However, I now feel my father 'arranged' to have my sister find that picture and give it to me."   *B. L. H.*

8

ADVICE AND HELP FROM THE DEAD

IN THE PREVIOUS chapter, we saw how the deceased soul's natural care for those left behind can lead to reassurance and consolation. In a similar way, those on the other side can offer guidance and direction. A broad array of help is possible, ranging from financial assistance to career advice to relationship counseling to health suggestions. Sometimes the guidance that seems to be coming from the spirit world is so specific that it can be readily checked out. When confirmation of its accuracy occurs, it is powerful evidence for a life beyond. Our first story is an excellent example.

GRANDFATHER PAYS THE MOVERS

The incident related here occurred during a time of pressing need for my correspondent and her family. Her grandfather's intervention brought material relief, as enduring love inspired joy and blessed ness.

''This experience happened in the mid-1930s. My grandfather, mother, sister, and I had all been living together. Times were hard; there were no government-assistance programs such as we have today.

''Grandfather was a kind man, very clean and helpful around the house in any way he was able to be. One year, just before Christmas, he died after a short illness. Our lease expired the following May, and to cut expenses we decided to move to smaller accommodations. Of course, there was the cost of moving and the medical bills to be paid. We were expecting the movers at eight o'clock one morning. Everything was packed, except for our beds.

"I awoke early that morning, feeling a 'presence.' Then I saw my grandfather standing by my bed, looking like his flesh-and-blood self, dressed as he usually was around the house. He proceeded to tell me—although I heard no voice—that he didn't want us to leave without the twenty dollars that he had put on the ledge under the shelf in his clothes cupboard. He told me there were two ten-dollar bills rolled up together, his savings from gifts received on birthdays and other occasions. That was all he said.

"At this point my mother came in to call me. I told her that I had just seen her father, and he had given me a message. We went to the now-empty cupboard and raised the shelf; and yes, something fell out. And yes, it was the two ten-dollar bills rolled up together! We surely would have moved without them. The extra money, much needed at the time, paid the movers.

"How very wonderful it is, and what a blessing, to know that our departed loved ones can remain close to us and watch over us. Since I had always believed that they are near and continue to care for us, I had felt no fear or strangeness when I saw my grandfather. This, however, has been my only visual experience of contact with the deceased."   *R. S.*

This story provides a convincing picture of the continuing presence of the dead and their lasting concern for the living. The grandfather's solicitude for his family, along with his unchanged appearance and attire, give the account a feeling of reality. Of course, the accuracy of the information furnishes powerful evidence that the experience was one of an actual communication from the departed one.

Another noteworthy element here is the practicality of the help received. The family didn't need a theoretical discussion of the nature of life or what it is like to die. They needed money, and that is what they got. The grandfather recognized this need and took simple, direct action to meet it.

This report also serves as a good example of several features we will come upon throughout this chapter. Each of the stories that follows shows that the deceased continue to be present with us and to know of our needs. Their love survives, and so they desire to help us with our difficulties. At least in some cases, they are able to provide us with practical, effective guidance and assistance. The enduring ability of the dead to offer aid to their loved ones is one of the most encouraging messages to be found in all the material I have received.

Assistance in the realm of money requirements is one important area. Most of us are at least somewhat mindful of the financial welfare of those about whom we care. I have received several reports which, like our opening story, show that this natural concern does not end with death. The next account introduces us to a soul who provided his wife with useful guidance that made a real difference. My correspondent's husband was aware of her need, he continued to be there for her, and he was able to give her the necessary aid.

LOVE CARRIES ON

This account shows both the desire and the ability of the departed to help the living meet their financial needs. In providing this aid, our narrator's husband not only assisted her materially, he left her with the uplifting knowledge that his love for her had not passed away.

*   *   *

"My husband had been a businessman, owning one-half of a florist firm. When he died, I became the owner of his share of the business. But disputes arose when my husband's partner tried to take over my portion of the enterprise, and the case was brought into court.

"When I was called to testify, an important question was raised. Not being sure of the answer, I prayed and mentally called to my departed husband, saying, 'Oh, Tom, if only you were here!' Suddenly I was inspired to say something that won the case for me. About the same time I heard his voice say, 'Atta girl, Alma, atta girl'—one of his favorite expressions of approval.

"I was thrilled to know that somewhere Tom was alive and still cared!" *A. R. C.*

In our next story, a similar type of guidance is given. Here we meet another woman who needed assistance in her financial affairs following her husband's death. In addition to recognizing his wife's need, the husband may have done a bit of "legwork" in order to locate an available source of aid for her. He was even able to select a good channel through which to get this information.

GUIDANCE FROM A DECEASED HUSBAND AND A FRIEND

In this account, our contributor gives us a clear sense of the protective presence of a soul who watches over the interests of people dear to them. The knowledge that this kind of aid is possible can be a source of much-needed comfort and encouragement to anyone left bereft by the death of a loved one.

"For some time after my late husband's death, I was having serious problems settling his estate. One Sunday morning, following services at the Spiritual Center, our organist approached me to tell me about a dream she had had a few nights previously.

"In the dream she had seen my husband and a close friend of hers. They had been together, engaged in animated and genial conversation, as if they were old friends. I inquired about this person, and the organist told me that for many years she had been a legal secretary working with a fine attorney—a man of great integrity and high reputation.

"I subsequently called this gentleman on the phone, and in just that one conversation he eased my anxiety and advised me what course to pursue. I never engaged any attorney, and eventually the estate was settled amicably. I couldn't help but feel that in some way my husband had been instrumental in getting me to contact this man."   *B. B.*

One of Edgar Cayce's own experiences provides another clear illustration that the deceased are aware of our financial concerns. This event—told to my husband and me by Mr. Cayce himself—is remarkable in that more than merely useful advice was received from the dead. The incident revealed that a soul can have the surprising ability to influence actual physical conditions in our world.

One day when he was especially concerned about money, Edgar Cayce was walking and praying in his garden. Suddenly his deceased mother appeared before him and asked him to hold out his hand. He did so, and she dropped a shiny new silver dollar into his palm. Then she reminded him to have faith, for the Lord would provide.

After telling us of this experience, Mr. Cayce opened the drawer of his desk and showed us not only the silver dollar, but also a "lodge pin" that had been fastened to his dead grandfather's burial suit! As to how this object had appeared in his drawer, he neither offered an explanation, nor did he seem to have one.

True, the actual amount of money Mrs. Cayce brought her son was not great. But she gave him a different type of assistance. Evidently she was aware of his financial worries and recognized that what he really needed was encouragement and faith. Far more valuable than the single dollar she handed him was the reassurance that he was being watched over and provided for.

Of course, money matters are not the only area of life for which the departed can offer advice. A second category is assistance related to vocational concerns. Several stories have come my way which illustrate just how useful the deceased can be in helping loved ones deal with career problems.

A PROPHECY OF A NEW CAREER

A good example of career guidance comes from one of Edgar Cayce's dreams. He received accurate information about a job that had been offered to a young friend. The incident showed that the young man's father was still interested in and aware of his son's career opportunities.

In this dream Edgar Cayce was talking with a deceased man who had been a fellow member of his church. This man spoke about his son, who had just gotten out of the army. He told Cayce that his son would be better off if he left the bank (where he had been employed before his military stint) and accepted the offer of a new job at a motion-picture house.

The day after having this dream, Mr. Cayce took a deposit to the young man's bank. He and Cayce were close friends, and Cayce inquired about his return from the army. His friend said that he had just gotten back the night before and expected to remain at the bank. Cayce then suggested that they meet at his office to discuss this decision.

When they got together later on, the young man told Cayce that during his return trip from Washington he had stopped in Atlanta and had been offered a job as manager of a motion-picture theater there. After thinking it over, he had sent a letter rejecting the offer. Mr. Cayce told the young man of his dream experience and advised him to take the new job, which he did.

A subsequent psychic reading identified the purpose of this dream: to show that love has the power to transcend even death; for love is a quality of the soul which never dies. In this case, the love was expressed as a father's desire to give his son helpful advice on choosing an occupation. Certainly this is a type of guidance that many living parents would seek to impart to their children.

It is certainly normal for us to care about the ability of our loved ones to earn a living. Since the dead do live on, it is only to be expected that they, too, would share this same concern. Sometimes, as in the story of Cayce's young friend, it is manifested as assistance in the choice of a career. In other cases, it takes the form of useful advice on the day-to-day details of job performance. This type of guidance is illustrated in our next two reports.

A KISS FOR ONE, CORRECTION FOR ANOTHER

In this account my correspondent tells of a deceased man who continued to be available for his family. There is a feeling here of a powerful individual presence, including a persistent desire to see the specific tasks of the family business carried out properly.

''A deceased friend of ours who had been in the nursery business appeared many times to his wife and daughter, giving them advice about both the business and their home. One morning his wife awakened with the very real feeling of his presence, emphasized by a kiss planted firmly on her lips. She knew he was there!

"His daughter, in sorrow, called to her father one evening. Suddenly she was aware of his presence. Then she saw him and heard him admonish her, saying, 'You're overwatering the palms. They will die!'

"This message, the daughter said, was typical of her father." *U. J.*

THOUGHTFULNESS LIVES ON

Sometimes the job-related guidance from the deceased is especially specific, practical, and accurate information. Perhaps the best example I have ever heard was from my friend Gladys Davis Turner, longtime secretary to Edgar Cayce and close friend of the Cayce family. In her capacity as secretary, Gladys stenographically recorded and then typed most of the readings Edgar Cayce gave. After his death she continued to play an important part in the A.R.E.'s work of preserving and documenting the readings.

Gladys' story concerns the thoughtfulness—even from the other side—of her deceased husband Al. The incident dramatically showed her that the dead have the ability to know of our problems and to help us find the solutions to them. This is a story of the lasting considerateness of a departed soul toward the person he had loved in life.

In the wee hours of the morning of her birthday, Gladys Davis Turner thought of her deceased husband. He had always been so very attentive to her, and she found herself missing him dreadfully. Unable to go back to sleep, she arose and scrubbed the kitchen floor.

That morning, at the A.R.E., while working in the files of the Cayce readings, Gladys discovered that a page was missing. She searched everywhere but was unsuccessful in finding it.

Suddenly she heard her husband's voice telling her where it was. He gave her the case number of the reading under which it had been erroneously filed. When she looked there, she found the missing sheet.

This experience made her feel less lonely, for it proved that in reality her husband was still in touch with her. Indeed, there is no death nor separation, even after the physical has passed away. Gladys has since crossed over, and I am sure her husband met her on the shore of the great river between our life here and the life hereafter.

The helpful advice we can receive from those who have gone on is not limited to any particular area of life. Any aspect of our existence that is important to us can be of interest to those who care about us, and this continues to be true even after the demise of the body. A third sphere into which this concern on our behalf naturally extends is our relationships with others. Our next story gives us a powerful illustration of just how valuable the help of the departed can be in this area.

A TALE OF HORROR AND MIRACLES

Here our contributor introduces us to a persistent, caring presence whose guidance, encouragement, and sense of humor provided a family with much-needed support during a long-term period of trial.

"I have been blessed in this lifetime with four beautiful children and the ability to manage my own successful business. But two years ago my physical world fell apart when I found out that my second husband had been sexually abusing two of my three daughters. He had abused the elder girl for five years and the younger one, aged thirteen, for six months.

"The younger girl eventually came to me with this incredible account of horror. At the same time, she told me that she was being helped by a friend of the family. This friend—a man who had passed over to the other side a few years before—had finally convinced her to tell me, not only for her own sake, but also for her sister's. He assured her that he would be with her at all times and that he would help me to deal with the situation and the authorities.

"What followed was a year of hell and miracles. Our departed friend was with us at every step, from our running and hiding to our final contact with the district attorney's office. He supported us spiritually, and he also helped us reach concrete decisions about finding the right lawyer and obtaining physical evidence. Throughout the ordeal he kept reassuring us that things were going to work out for the best.

"There never was a doubt in my mind that our friend was there with us. My younger daughter was able to tell me explicit details of business transactions I had had with him before he passed over; there was no way she could have gotten this information other than through him.

"This friend has continued to help us in matters unrelated to the difficulty that first brought us his aid. On one recent occasion, he told my daughter not to drive anywhere that day. He said that there was going to be a big accident on a highway near us and that she might be involved. She took his advice. The next day there was a major accident, causing the deaths of several people, on the highway he had named.

"Our departed friend has helped us not only with his tremendous insight, but also with a terrific sense of humor. When we asked if there was a God—the Life Force of all that is—he jokingly answered, 'I never saw Him myself!' In the guidance he offers, our friend stresses honesty, loving each other, and recognizing the God in all of us."

J. S. and V. C.

*   *   *

Our next report is from a man who received help with
what is, thank heaven, a more common type of interpersonal problem than the previous account. The story
tells of a soul who recognizes her grandson's need for
reconciliation and sends him a symbolic message that
prompts him to seek it. Her action illustrates the ability
of the dead to know of our relationships with others, and
their willingness to help us make constructive changes
in those relationships if necessary.

DIRECTION FROM GRANDMA

In this story, our narrator's grandmother gives him a
type of aid that would greatly enrich the lives of so many
of us—the motivation to transform animosity into
friendship. We have here a clear portrait of the lasting
closeness that can exist between two people, even after
one of them has died.

"My mother's mother, Grandma Bea, was closer to me
than any other woman in my life, next to my mom. This
closeness lasted until my grandmother's death. Even after she passed on, there were two or three occasions on
which we met in a dream.

"During one of these visits she gave me several
bank books and told me they were my inheritance. I
was surprised at the sum of money they represented. It
seemed so large! Grandma Bea asked me if I would
please give just a little bit of the money to my Uncle
Jackie, who was in need. I really didn't want to, but I
also didn't want to disappoint her, and I realized I
could easily afford to help my uncle. Then I awakened.

"Grandma Bea had never known Uncle Jackie in life.
She died before I married, and Jackie is my wife's uncle.
Some time before my dream, Uncle Jackie and I had had

a terrible fight, and we hadn't yet resolved it. I listened to Grandma, of course, and went to see Uncle Jackie to apologize. I learned that he had visited my home two days earlier, also to apologize! Unfortunately, no one had been home to greet him.''   *H. G.*

A fourth basic aspect of life in which my correspondents have received practical, helpful guidance from the dead is the area of physical health. The following account gives a straightforward and convincing example of this type of aid. Though the identity of the doctor described here and the source of his information are not definitely established, the positive results obtained by following his treatment show that the advice he transmitted was indeed valid.

A PRESCRIPTION FROM ANOTHER REALM

This story brings us the hopeful message that in times of difficulty we have more help available to us than is generally realized. Although there is some ambiguity about the exact identity of the one giving advice, it could very well be a soul whose healing work continues from the other side. Just how important this hopeful message can be—particularly to those who are in pain—is shown in my correspondent's closing expression of appreciation.

''My husband was suffering from excruciating pain in his right knee. It seemed that nothing was able to help him or to cure his condition.

''One night, in a dream, a doctor in a gray pin-striped suit appeared to him. The physician stroked his goatee a bit and thoughtfully said, 'No! No!' followed by 'Yes! Yes!' He then proceeded to give my husband detailed instructions for a course of treatment, including medications he should take in order to be healed.

"After having this dream, my husband discussed the prescribed treatment with several doctors. Their reaction was a definite 'No.' Some time later, he met with a friend of his, a Lebanese neuropsychiatrist and physician, who heartily endorsed the treatment recommended by the dream doctor. To make a long story short, the dream remedy worked, and the condition was completely cured.

"This incident reminded me of Edgar Cayce's advice that we should never forget the doctor within. Whether the doctor in my husband's dream was a representation of the Divine within himself or an actual physician from another dimension, we do not know. But, in either case, this experience was truly a great and blessed one."

F. M.

Our next account describes a series of healing-related dreams with a new wrinkle: the departed's actions do not so much bring advice that is of direct benefit to the dreamer, but instead the deceased conveys information that will help the dreamer help others. In describing how this teamwork operates, our story underscores the effectiveness of prayer and indicates that this effectiveness is recognized by beings in the spirit world.

A COMPANION IN HEALING PRAYER

This report introduces us to an engaging man who undergoes a dramatic change. The first time he appears in a dream, our contributor's uncle is sorrowful and afraid; later, he is joyful, with enough strength and self-confidence to want to be of service to others. He regains his natural kindness and generosity on the other side of life.

"Uncle Morris, my father's sister's husband, was always kind and gentle with me, and he had a great sense of humor. He did use 'foul language' very frequently, but he had a way of making it seem funny and natural. He was a generous man, uneducated, who had been born in Europe and raised partly in the United States. He spoke with a decidedly Jewish accent.

"I saw Uncle Morris about once a week during my youth, and in my teens I worked for him, selling hot dogs at his business place in Coney Island. I did this for four consecutive summers and became quite fond of him. We never had any conflicts nor harsh words. But I never did get to feel as close to him as I might have.

"After coming to live in Hawaii, I didn't see Uncle Morris for at least twelve years and seldom thought of him. He was still living in New York, and we lost contact with each other. Then my mother told me that he was suffering from inoperable brain cancer and was in a coma. I started praying for him each day and continued to do so for what seemed like a long period, though I don't recall how much time really passed.

"Then one night, in my sleep I found myself kneeling at Uncle Morris's bedside, while he cried and sobbed for a long time. In the dream, I didn't seem to realize he was ill. I wanted to touch him. He became very upset at this, so I asked him what was wrong. He stopped crying long enough to tell me that he didn't want me to catch what he had. Unaware of what he was talking about but understanding that he was under great stress, I told him it was impossible for me to catch what he had. I kissed him, and he seemed horrified. Then I held him until his fears and tears subsided.

"In the days following this dream, I continued to pray for Uncle Morris, and we visited once again in my sleep. This time he told me he was fine, he no longer had a problem, and I needn't be concerned on his account. I later learned that during this period he had regained consciousness and had gone home to die. I kept praying for him up to the time of his passing and beyond.

"Over the nine years since his death Uncle Morris has come into my dreams about seven or eight times. On the first occasion, he appeared in lovely green fields. He seemed quite happy, and we spoke about various family members. It was all very pleasant.

"After this experience, in subsequent dream visits, he started to bring family members to me. He always walked a step or two behind them. The first person he brought was my sister, who was alive. But, as I later learned, she had been hospitalized at the time Uncle Morris brought her to see me. When I discovered this, I realized that in bringing others into my dreams with him Uncle Morris may have been alerting me to a need for prayer.

"The next time I saw him in a dream he was with his daughter, who had died a dozen years before him. They were holding hands, and in front of them stood my Aunt Bertha, who was then living in Florida. We exchanged pleasantries, and I awoke.

"I began praying for Aunt Bertha every day and tried to get in touch with her in Florida, but I was unable to reach her. I continued to pray for her, and I called other relatives in an attempt to find out how she was. After about a week, I finally discovered that she had undergone open-heart surgery right around the night of my dream. By the time I learned this, Aunt Bertha was recovering nicely! Apparently my prayers for her had been helpful.

"Uncle Morris has appeared in several more of my dreams, sometimes with family members whom he barely knew. I came to understand that each of these visits was a request for prayer. I haven't seen him for about a year now. Peculiarly, in all our meetings since his death, I haven't once realized that he has passed on. Perhaps this is because he really is still alive—only in a different body!''

H. G.

HELPFUL PHYSICAL ACTIONS BY THE DEAD

We have now seen many reports in which the deceased have imparted valuable *information* and *guidance* to the living. If such advice were all the help the dead could give us, that in itself would be wonderful. But the ability of the departed to be of assistance in our lives goes beyond even this. Several of the stories I have received tell of incidents in which souls on the other side of life have in some way *directly affected conditions in the physical*. As one example of such an experience, we have the deceased Mrs. Cayce's gift of an actual silver dollar to her son Edgar.

The accounts in the remainder of this chapter relate events in which the dead have taken effective action upon the physical world in order to benefit the health of the living. This material suggests that the different planes of life are not as completely separate from each other as we might think. The ability of some souls to bridge the gap between dimensions gives us yet another indication that death is not the end of life.

The closeness of the spirit world to ours is shown in the next story, which was sent to me by the same woman whose husband was cured of a painful knee ailment through the help of a dream doctor. Here my correspondent herself receives aid from someone in another realm. Again, it is not certain that the helper is a soul recently departed from physical life. But whatever plane this woman saw into, her experience holds out the encouraging message that it is possible for us to receive assistance from more worlds than just our own.

HELP FROM THE SPIRIT WORLD

In this report our narrator is given a glimpse of a world of awesome peacefulness and beauty, and her pain is alleviated through actual physical contact with a helpful being in that world. The account provides us with a vivid description of the powerful emotional impact this experience had.

"Some time ago I had an operation for a diaphragmatic hernia. I was in a great deal of pain for a number of days, and the only way I could be comfortable was to lie on my back. But the nurses kept insisting that I turn over onto my right side, to keep fluid from collecting in my lung. That was the side of my incision, however, and for several days it was impossible for me to lie on it. Two nights before I was due to go home, after having been given pain medication, I finally felt able to turn myself over onto my right side. I did so and was immediately asleep.

"Several hours later I awoke and found the pain intolerable. The room was completely dark, but I had a sense that someone was there with me. Thinking it must be a nurse, I asked, 'Could you please turn me over?'

"A child's voice said, 'I'll turn you over.' Two arms went underneath me, and instantly I was on my back. I looked around, and there stood a young girl of perhaps twelve or thirteen. She had on a grayish cape and held a reed in her right hand. It had large leaves, which were moving in a breeze.

"A whole incredible picture was in front of me. I

was looking into another world and was awed by its tranquility. The girl was standing in what appeared to be a river bed, which had lots of stones in it. Still farther back was a desert with a hill in the center. The girl sat down on a rock and put her hands under her chin, and we gazed at each other. No audible words were spoken; we just shared inaudible spirit communication. It was so beautiful!

"Then, from a distance, a woman's voice said, 'Don't frighten ill people.'

" 'I'm not frightening her,' the girl responded. After a few moments a soft light began to wash over everything. The girl jumped up from her rock and said, 'I have to go now.'

" 'Don't go, please don't go,' I begged. But she turned and started running toward the hill.

" 'I have to,' she said. The whole picture faded, and I was left by myself in a dark hospital room. The experience had been truly awe-inspiring."   *F. M.*

Throughout this chapter we have seen that love is not extinguished by the death of the body. Those who care about us in life continue to care for us after they have passed on, and in at least some cases they are able to express their tender feelings by offering us guidance and physical help. This basic message is clearly shown in our two closing reports.

THE ROD OF HEALING

This heartening story tells of a sister's love that endured even after years of separation by death. Out of that love there arose some remarkably effective aid: real physical healing was brought to my correspondent from the other side of life.

*   *   *

"A long time ago a young sister of mine died of peritonitis. Before going to bed on the night she passed away, I stood by the window, looking out. It was a very cold night, with snow on the ground. I awakened early the next morning, as the clock was striking the hour of five. Almost immediately I heard a voice say, 'If you had known that man at Virginia Beach, your sister would not have died.' This was repeated over and over again. At that time I had not yet met Edgar Cayce, although I had heard about him.

"I grieved for my sister for many years. One night, after I had gone to bed feeling ill, she appeared to me. She had a long rod in her hand. She thrust it down my throat three times, and I was well.

"As my sister began to leave, I asked her to stay awhile, because I had some questions for her. But she replied, 'I must be about my Father's business.' Then she was gone.

"I later asked Mr. Cayce about the rod my sister had carried. He said, 'I think that was the healing rod.' "

R. L.

MY NIGHT NURSE—MY DEAD MOTHER!

This account is another in which we can see that the love of the departed for the living—in this case, a mother's devotion to her daughter—can remain alive for a long time. Our narrator's mother evidently stayed close to her child for a number of years, watching over her and displaying a persistent, tender care for her health.

"Among the experiences with the departed that have involved members of my family is one that affected me quite personally. At one point in my life I was seriously ill indeed, with pneumonia, and confined to my bed. My medication had to be given on a very regular schedule, which necessitated awakening me during the night. One night I drowsily accepted my medicine and went back to sleep.

"But the next morning, both my adoptive mother and the nurse insisted that they had slept through the night. In fact, they were quite upset about it. Then they saw that the dosage had been marked off as given, and I got a joint lecture: 'Don't be getting up and wandering around alone; we'll have to put you in the hospital.'

"At that point I explained what had happened. Without prompting I described the woman who had given me my medicine. Everyone fell silent.

"My natural mother had died when I was so young that I cannot remember her, and I had been adopted by her best friend. When I finished the description of my midnight nurse, my adoptive mom informed me that the woman who had ministered to me was Myrtle— my mother for the first two-and-one-half years of my life!

"I have no explanation for this experience. Can dreams and visions dispense a dose of medicine? I do not know. I do not know that there are no limits to love."

C. P. P.

There is something truly awe-inspiring about these stories in which the deceased are apparently able to have a helpful influence directly into the physical world. This is guidance and support in its most potent expression. But even when we do not get such an impressive display of evidence, even when no dramatic sign is forthcoming, we still can get exactly what we need from souls offering help from the spirit world. It may be merely a hunch or feeling whose source seems to come mysteriously from beyond ourselves. The guidance may come from a dream contact or a fleeting apparition. The point is for us, here on this side of life, to stay open and sensitive to the loving help that is being presented to us from the deceased whenever we face a difficulty. That is a comforting fact to remember.

9

WHEN THINGS GO WRONG

THERE ARE OCCASIONS, of course, when contacts with the deceased are troublesome. I have had a number of personal experiences of this type. For example, on one occasion, after buying a new home, my husband and I discovered we had an unexpected guest: a soul who had become attached to an area of the house and was unwilling or unable to leave. Attachments of this sort are probably the basic reason behind most hauntings.

The home was in Sherman Oaks, California. It was practically new and came up for sale because the owner had recently died. The first time we saw the house we loved it, and we bought it at once. Shortly thereafter we moved in.

The very first night that we slept in the master bedroom we felt uncomfortable. Something was wrong! I called the woman from whom we had purchased the house and asked her very bluntly if anyone had died in that room. She hesitated a moment and then said, "Well, yes. Margaret, who owned the house with me, died there. She was ill with cancer for six months in that room and fought death every step of the way." I knew then that Margaret was still there.

The next night, when I felt her presence, I told her that she had died and we were now the new owners of the house. I then told her that God had another home for her, and she would find it if she would pray and ask the way. Then my husband and I also prayed for her. Margaret never again came back to that home in the ten years we lived there.

This story is an example of a disturbing encounter with the deceased. Up to this point we have been exploring mainly positive experiences of contact with the dead. On the whole, the stories I have heard and read for decades indicate that these cases are the most common type. But, as the account of my haunted bedroom shows, there can be problems on the other side of life, just as there are in this world. In Margaret's case, perhaps the trouble arose from her determined fight for physical life; when the time for her transition came, she may not have been ready to accept her new condition and to move on. This is one of the ways in which a soul can become earthbound. Spiritual growth is hindered because the soul is unable to make use of the opportunities and learn the special lessons death ordinarily makes available.

An important feature of Margaret's story is that her difficulty was overcome in the end. This is what is possible for *any* soul that is confused or troubled. In the material that follows, we will meet some deceased persons who do not realize they have died. We will encounter other souls, like Margaret, who have become bound to various elements of the earth plane. We will also see some who have moved away from the earth and entered different places of abode, unpleasant ones that might be thought of as "hell." We will also get a glimpse of the extreme misery suffered by souls in outer darkness. But keep in mind that none of these situations is permanent. Problems on the other side *do* have solutions. There is always hope.

THE FAILURE TO REALIZE DEATH
HAS OCCURRED

As mentioned in Chapter 4, the Cayce material tells us that it is not uncommon for a soul to fail to realize the body has died: ". . . many an individual has remained in that [which is] called death for what ye call *years* without realizing it was dead!" (1472-2) This lack of awareness may be one of the factors that keeps ghosts such as Margaret from leaving the material sphere. Not knowing the body has met its demise, these souls may remain in locations they had inhabited during physical life.

In Chapter 5 we saw that souls who have recently crossed over typically go through a period of unconsciousness or disorientation on the other side. Not recognizing that one has died could be simply one form of this common confusion. For various reasons, some souls take a long time to pass through this disorientation phase—although admittedly "time" probably has a different meaning to those in the spirit world. As an example of the "time" that may be involved, in one reading Cayce made reference to a man who had died eight years earlier, saying: "Now, this is very interesting, to know that [this soul] has just come to the realization of being in the borderland." (3817-1)

One possible reason for the inability to understand that death has occurred could be a prolonged, resolute struggle to hold onto physical life, as we saw in Margaret's case. In other instances, the cause might lie in fear of the afterlife or disbelief that we survive physical death. For some individuals, it might simply be that the transition was very sudden and completely unexpected. This could well be the case in our next story.

A HUSBAND EXPLAINS HIS DEATH

In this account my correspondent plainly communicates a sense of her husband's disorientation and failure to realize he had died. Perhaps this lack of awareness was the reason for his persistent presence.

"My husband was killed in a plane crash in 1972. After his death I sensed his presence with me at times and prayed for him. Often when I was out, I even expected to see him walking down the other side of the street. Then one day, while I was meditating, he came to me and told me that he had not died instantly, but had felt the pain of the accident.

"I have no proof, but I had the feeling my husband was in 'hell' for eight years, not knowing where he was or even realizing that he was dead. Though I was not brought up Roman Catholic, I do believe that some great knowledge is shown in their High Mass for the departed. Had I known of this rite at the time of my husband's death, more could have been done to release him into the light."   *V. B.*

In emotional tones, this story is much different from our earlier, happier reports of the continuing presence of the deceased. In most of those accounts, joy and peace were communicated by the dead. In this one, the dominant feeling is of the departed soul's confusion.

But this story, too, has its positive side, which is shown in the suggestion that the husband's period in "hell" was limited to eight years. At the end of that time, his soul was evidently able to move into the more typical growth-fostering experiences on the other side of life. Notice our narrator's statement of faith in the power of prayer to help the soul enter the light more quickly. This gives us yet another reason to pray for our loved ones who have gone on.

THE JUDGMENT OF THE SOUL

What, exactly, determines the type of experience any particular soul will enter into at the end of life? The Cayce readings tell us that at some point after a physical body passes away, the life that has just ended is examined. This evaluation largely establishes what kind of experiences the soul will undergo in the next world. According to the readings, the judgment of the soul is not performed by any outside agent. Rather, each lifetime is evaluated by the individual's own conscience; the standards that are used are the knowledge and opportunity that had been available during that lifetime.

Most important is the soul's own evaluation of the actions it took and the ideals it chose to pursue in material life. Optimally the soul's ideals were patterned after God—the Giver of life—and that which is constructive and creative, otherwise what can we expect the experience to be when the soul sheds its material consciousness and stands exposed before its own conscience, its God? Will the soul, like Adam and Eve, find itself naked before God—and terribly ashamed?

What the soul discovers in itself during this examination will reveal the type of afterlife experiences it needs for spiritual growth. The Cayce readings mention three basic alternatives. In most instances the afterlife experiences will be positive and stimulating. But for some individuals, a period in an unpleasant dimension may be required to teach an essential lesson. And—extremely rarely, according to the Cayce readings—there are some cases in which over *many* lifetimes a soul will have made no progress toward its goal of reunion with the Father; such a soul may lose its personal identity and be reabsorbed into the Creative Force, or God. Whichever of these three possibilities is necessary, that will be the experience the soul moves into after death.

Let us look more closely at the second alternative, as described by Cayce. His readings sometimes refer to a necessary period in unpleasant circumstances by using the phrase "banishment of a soul from its Maker." It could be applied to several of the stories I've collected—ones which show the deceased in realms where they are apparently without awareness of the closeness and love of God. But this banishment is not eternal; it is part of the soul's effort to work out its own salvation. Eventually, the "banished" soul will find its way back to its Creator.

Thus, there is no eternal damnation. Whatever the soul meets in the afterlife has a role in its return to God. As in material life, any problem encountered after death has a positive function in spiritual development. Its purpose is to teach us, by helping us recognize and overcome our mistakes. When this function has been fulfilled, the soul is able to move beyond the difficulty—either by entering another dimension on the other side or by re-entering physical life through reincarnation.

ATTACHMENTS TO THE EARTH PLANE

Each individual's choices during physical life lead to certain experiences after death, as determined by the soul's self-judgment. Usually these experiences involve different, expanded opportunities for spiritual growth. But it is possible for the soul's normal advancement in the afterlife to be hindered by overly strong ties to the material world.

The period during which the departed soul is active in the earth plane can be a positive time of growth through helpful interaction with others, both alive and dead. But, unfortunately, this isn't always what happens. After their transition, some souls find themselves "earth-bound"—a term meaning tied to the material world in unproductive ways. Instead of freedom and spiritual advancement, they experience stagnation. Their development is delayed because they are unable to use the special opportunities death ordinarily provides.

There is a big difference between a soul that is earthbound and one that has the freedom which the dead can enjoy while still conscious of the earth plane. Which experience will each of us find in the afterlife? That depends entirely upon how we choose to live now.

The manner of life one presently lives either produces earthly attachments or prevents their formation. When earthly attachments form, they are the results of the individual's decision to make material things so important that they continue to hold the soul after death, interfering with its normal development. Whenever a deceased person is limited on the other side—bound by earthly ties—it is because of choices made along the way.

In the first story of this chapter, we saw one type of earthly tie. There we met a soul with a strong attachment to a specific place. Exactly *how* such a bond might be formed is considered in our next account. This report begins with a dream that seems to be precognitive, alerting my correspondent that there might come some spiritual work to be done with a certain neighbor. But the primary message of this story is that a soul's attachment to a place does not arise out of blind fate. Any restrictive tie can be avoided.

HELPING A NEIGHBOR MOVE ON

Whether or not the deceased will be bound to a specific place is determined by a decision of the individual soul: to remain in darkness or to move into the light. The contributor of this account helped one of her neighbors as he was facing this decision.

"On May 20, 1984, I dreamed that a neighbor and I were in small boats in the middle of a river, near the tangle of a fallen tree. We were lowering ropes into the water next to the tree, doing some kind of work—what, exactly, was not clear. Water, in my dreams, represents the spiritual aspect of life. The neighbor was one I knew only well enough to see that he was a nervous and angry old man with a history of heart problems. This dream did not mean anything to me at the time I had it.

"On November 6, 1984, this neighbor had a noisy argument with his son outside his home. The older man tried to go into his house, but his son jumped into his way and taunted him about needing a doctor. The old man saw me and asked that someone call the police, which I did. Later that day, the old man had heart attack and died.

"That evening I found him [with clairvoyant sight] standing in the road, looking toward his house. I told him, telepathically, that the house was no longer an appropriate concern of his and that I would be glad to talk with him about what to do next.

"He stayed there with me through the evening and into the night, so I spoke with him about attachment and about the spiritual self. I told him I had read about looking for a light and going toward it—and that if he did, someone would come to help him.

"Some time later friendly entities did come to help my neighbor, but he still wouldn't leave. I thought it would probably be all right for him to rest and think about his decision awhile. I told him emphatically, however, that he should not become attached to that place. Throughout this period, beginning when I had first psychically seen my neighbor that evening, he had been surrounded by darkness.

"Late that night, he made the decision to try love;

and immediately a light appeared on the horizon! The Lord gives us many opportunities to make the right choices. I feel that the moment my neighbor had made his loving decision, the friendly beings helped him move toward the light. Shortly thereafter they all left together. Later experiences showed me that all was well with him.''   *D. B.*

Earthly ties other than just those involving specific locations can affect an individual after death. Judging from the Cayce material, one of the most common ties results from abnormal appetites of the flesh. Uncontrolled desires can impel people to act in certain ways during physical life. These drives can continue to influence the soul's activities after death, keeping it bound to the earth.

ABNORMAL APPETITES

Sometimes, as Cayce's consciousness left the body to give a psychic reading, he would have visions of the nonphysical side of the earth dimension. Some of the scenes he witnessed involved people with uncontrolled physical appetites. For example, during some of these out-of-body travels, Cayce saw the distress of deceased souls who had been heavy smokers, alcoholics, over-indulgers in food, and people with uncontrolled sex drives. Evidently these hungers can persist beyond death and cause limitation and suffering. After their transition, individuals with such habits often remain about the earth in an effort to satisfy their appetites.

At various times, Cayce commented on the afflictions faced by excessive smokers. After death, those addicted to nicotine often hang around bars or night clubs which are heavy with smoke, trying to get a little relief from their desire for tobacco. Deceased alcoholics are sometimes seen by clairvoyants and psychics in similar surroundings, frustrated in attempts to gratify cravings by inhaling the breath of living drinkers. The soul that once had an abnormal appetite for food may find itself after death hovering around bakeries and restaurants, trying to satisfy its hunger by taking in the odor of foods. And the person who had an uncontrolled sex drive may after death visit houses of ill repute in fruitless attempts to fulfill excessive urges.

Such scenes show another way in which we create our own experiences in the next world. Extreme appetites like these are built during physical life as the result of individual choices. Their hindering effects—just like the helpful effects of our more positive, loving decisions—can stay with the soul long after the death of the body.

In some cases, our excessive cravings can persist even into future incarnations, where they produce karmic effects. This is possible, for example, with people who have ungoverned sex drives.

One karmic result of excessive sexual activity, according to the Cayce information, can be epilepsy. In a case involving this ailment, Edgar Cayce had a vision of a horrible, drooling creature coming to possess the sufferer. This monster, Cayce said, was a symbol of the person's own lust—a carry-over from more than one lifetime.

The readings on reincarnation describe ways that certain physical conditions in the present can often be traced back to a person's activities during previous incarnations. For instance, obesity may be directly due to a glandular condition or to overeating in the present, but these immediate causes might themselves be the karmic result of past-life choices. Potentially, there are several plausible explanations that involve reincarnation. The overeating could be the continuation of a habit begun during an earlier lifetime. On the other hand, it may be that during a former incarnation the person had insufficient food, perhaps starving to death, and the present tendency to retain calories is a reaction to that experience. Or maybe the person who now has trouble controlling his or her weight had, in a previous lifetime, made fun of others who were obese. The present condition would be karmic, quite possibly with the purpose of teaching that individual needed tolerance and compassion.

Some cases of homosexuality could have a similar explanation. In one Cayce life reading a present-day homosexual was told that in a previous lifetime as a heterosexual he had made fun of homosexuals. In readings for other homosexuals, the origin of their preference is described as the result of a change in gender from one lifetime to the next. A person who had been a man in a recent lifetime and who came back in a female body this time might find that the sexual preference from the past continued on, producing lesbianism.

These are just some illustrations of how difficulties can arise in accordance with the law of cause and effect, or karma. There are no injustices in life, the Cayce material tells us. In both this world and the afterlife, we experience the results of our own choices. If, for instance, someone is falsely arrested or falsely executed in one life, we should consider how it may well be a karmic effect carried over from a previous incarnation. This is also true of birth defects, physical abnormalities, or anything else considered unfortunate.

It is important to remember that the unpleasant conditions we meet, whether during physical life or after it has ended, are not permanent. They are simply part of the soul's education, teaching us the lessons we need to learn in order to make our way back to God. Our karma is really an opportunity for soul growth!

PLANES OF HELL AND OUTER DARKNESS

In Chapter 5 we saw that in most cases the departed spend a certain amount of time in the earth plane—in a dimension of consciousness from which they can still readily perceive the physical world. Later, they move on to other realms. Similarly, some souls whose choices have produced difficulties for themselves in the afterlife remain attached to the earth, while others meet the results of their misguided actions in other dimensions. What are those other realms?

Our next story describes what one such dimension might be like. We cannot be sure whether the dream related here is a vision of an actual nonearthly plane or simply a symbolic warning against a possibly harmful mental pattern. But in either case, it illustrates how we ourselves can build our own unpleasant experiences in the afterlife. The world pictured in this account is limited, narrow, and stagnant—just like the materialistic outlook about which my correspondent felt the dream cautioned him.

A BUSINESSMAN'S HELL

This dream showed our contributor a world that nobody would ever want to visit. The hopeful part of the account is the last paragraph, where we can see that the narrator recognizes and is willing to change the habit of mind against which his vision warns.

"In a dream I was on a train. I knew that everyone there was dead, and we were all going to our places in the afterlife. Most of us on the train were ordinary-looking people. A few priests and nuns were also present.

"As we approached a train depot, the conductor announced the name of the station as 'Heaven.' Everyone stood up, preparing to get off. Then the voice over the loudspeaker said, 'All those who deem themselves worthy of Heaven may get off.' Hearing that, I promptly sat down! Only a few priests and nuns left the train at 'Heaven.'

"The next minute I found myself in what appeared to be an endless room, in which there seemed to be a large crowd of people. They were divided into groups of ten, standing in circles and holding hands. I myself was in one of these circles. We could speak only to the person on our right, and we could only repeat what had been told us by the person on our left.

"Suddenly a ripple of excitement ran through the crowd. The man on my left said to me, 'One-point-two percent.' I passed this on to the person on my right. He, too, became very excited. I asked him why there was such a stir over a simple statement. He answered, 'Man, that is the first new thing we have heard in a thousand years.'

"I might explain that in my waking life I am a businessman with several offices, and much of my activity is concerned with money. I realized my dream experience was telling me that my interests, up to that time, had all been materially oriented and that I should place more emphasis on my spiritual development." *R. M.*

There are, of course, a great many different types of mistakes a person might make in physical life, so there is a wide variety of lessons for individual souls to assimilate in the afterlife. We might, therefore, expect a number of different realms the soul could move into after death, each with conditions especially suited to teaching a specific lesson. Edgar Cayce had a number of experiences that indicated as much.

DIMENSIONS OF HELL

Edgar Cayce saw into many nonearthly planes as he entered the trance state to give readings. During these experiences he was able to view conditions in these nonphysical worlds and the lessons departed souls were learning in them. Some of the realms he described could well be considered dimensions of "hell."

On several of the planes Cayce saw beings with grossly distorted forms which appeared to be emphasizing the wrong use of certain physical faculties in life. Some of the shapes were truly grotesque—people with immense stomachs, huge tongues, and other parts of the body greatly enlarged. Being trapped in this sort of form would make the soul acutely aware of its gluttony, misuse of the power of speech, or other physical failings. What better way could there be to call attention to one's transgressions!

One of the dimensions Cayce described was the abode of the egotist who felt he knew everything. After death, such a soul might find itself in a place where each person present had an enormous head. All the people in this world believed they knew everything. The result was that everyone there was talking, but no one was listening. What a hell that would be for an egotist!

The karma of extreme egotism might carry over into another physical life, causing the soul to be born into a hydrocephalic body. Through this experience the individual enters a situation in which he or she must listen to others, and in which he or she is completely helpless and has to be taken care of in every way. Thus the individual is given a chance to learn appreciation for others; but, even more important, to learn to listen.

Of all the planes of hell, perhaps the most dreadful is one that Jesus may have been referring to when He used the phrase "outer darkness" (Matthew 8:12). In a powerful vision of a soul in outer darkness, it was underscored for me the responsibility of each individual for his or her own actions and the extreme way in which our choices can build consequences that must be met. Sadly, these consequences are not always the ones we want or expect. I personally witnessed something of the anguish of souls in outer darkness. In my visionary dream experience I was forcefully struck by the depressing atmosphere of the scene. This atmosphere, the dark and gloomy water, and the forlorn voice of the soul I saw combined to create a feeling of utter desolation.

First, here is the background to my vision: A married man, with several children, fell in love with his secretary, who was also married. He was a teacher in the field of metaphysics and was fully aware of the meaning of the vows taken in marriage: ". . . 'til death do us part."

He and his secretary, who were very much in love, committed suicide together, even though both knew that killing oneself was wrong, especially in their case. Evidently they thought this action would bring them release from their vows and allow them to be together forever. When I heard what they had done, I began praying for them ardently.

One night as I was praying for them, I fell asleep and had a very vivid dream experience. In the dream it was nighttime. I saw the man standing alone by a large body of very dark water, surrounded by utter darkness. In the most pitiful human voice I have ever heard, he was calling out for his secretary—"Celia, Celia, Celia." Though they had committed suicide together, each was now completely alone.

I awakened from the dream and immediately began praying more fervently for those lost souls in outer darkness. This experience strengthened my realization that vows taken on the altar of God cannot be easily broken.

Admittedly, my visionary dream could lead us to believe that suicide produces a totally hopeless situation, leaving the soul in darkness forever. But I have had other experiences that show otherwise. One of these incidents is related below. A remarkable feature of this account is the accuracy of the psychic information given by Olga Worrell, one of the women in the story. This undeniable demonstration of extrasensory ability reassured me that Mrs. Worrell's psychic powers were on target and that someone dear to me had, in fact, been able to move into the light.

A PSYCHIC CONFIRMS THE POWER OF PRAYER

One day when I was in Virginia Beach visiting the A.R.E., I was invited to dinner at the home of Bob and Isabel Adriance. That evening they had other guests for dinner: Olga Worrell, a well-known psychic in America, and her husband, Ambrose.

After we had eaten, Olga said to me, "I see a large number of people from the other side standing around you. They want to thank you for your constant prayers for them."

When I asked her who was there, I was astonished to hear her identify nine people—each of whom was on my daily prayer list! Even the name Tante Bartetzko was given correctly. No one could guess that!

Then Olga said, "And your brother is here." I was truly amazed. My brother had committed suicide some years before. I had been praying for him nightly but had told no one outside the home about it.

Olga added, as if to console me, "He says to tell you it's all right. He is now with your grandmother, in the light." I found this information very reassuring, for if ever there was an angel on earth, my grandmother came very close to being one.

My experience contains an encouraging message for

us all: there are no problems in the afterlife without solutions; even a soul's stay in outer darkness is not permanent. It may take time, but liberation is possible. No matter what the problem or limitation may be—and this chapter has explored a number of troublesome experiences a soul may have inadvertently created for itself—there is always hope.

10

How We Can Help

I ONCE HAD an experience that clearly illustrates the theme of this chapter: souls on the other side are aware of our efforts on their behalf *and* they are responsive. These events from many years ago involved a dear, deceased friend who simply would not admit that he had passed on. This refusal limited his opportunity for advancement, and it caused his wife some uneasiness as well. But the problem proved to be solvable, and the incident leaves us with the encouraging truth that we can help our loved ones overcome their difficulties, even after death.

While living in Los Angeles, Bill and I had wonderful neighbors, particularly those who lived directly across the street from us. I had a special rapport with Don, the father of the family. Every Sunday morning as my husband and I left for church, we would see Don, busily clipping his hedges, and he would call out, "Don't forget to pray for me." This we faithfully did.

One day, without warning, Don suddenly died of a massive heart attack. Bill and I had moved to another state by that time, but we continued to pray for him.

About a year later we returned and visited Don's wife. In the course of our conversation, she told us that he was still there. No one had been able to sleep in his bed since his death. Those who tried always sensed another presence and felt someone seemingly attempting to push them out of the bed!

Don's wife then told me of a strange dream. In her dream, Don's brother, who had preceded him in death, was carrying her husband in his arms like a baby. He kept telling Don that he was dead and asking him to please open his eyes to the truth and go on from there. Don would open his eyes to peek for a moment and then quickly close them again, refusing to acknowledge his death. After relating this dream, the wife said that she felt his presence in the home constantly.

One day during a later visit, I asked if her husband was there at that moment. Her answer was, "Oh yes, he is here now!" I then requested that she let me speak to him alone.

When she left, I addressed him audibly, saying, "Don, you know me well. You know I would never lie to you. You had a heart attack one Sunday while clipping the hedges, and you died suddenly. That is why you are with your departed brother now, and he is trying to tell you to face the fact that you have passed away. Your body is dead, but your soul lives on!

"Your daughter is married now. Would it not be wonderful if you could come back as her child? But you must first recognize that you have crossed over and learn some other lessons. Only then will you be able to return.

"You know I never lied to you when we discussed religion, and I am being truthful now. So recognize where you are, so you will be able to come back again."

Don's wife reported to me soon thereafter that her husband was now gone.

This story shows the problem that can arise when a person either does not know that death has occurred or is unwilling to accept that it has. The account also shows two basic ways in which we can help the soul move beyond this obstacle. The first is through prayer. The difficulty the deceased sometimes have in realizing that they are dead is one important reason many religions teach us to pray for them. This is something we all should do. The second technique for aiding souls in this

situation is simply to inform them that they have passed
on. If we can get this message across, we may be able
to help them move on and resume their normal development.

But the possibility of helping the dead raises the question of whether communication with them is always beneficial. In some cases it can help the departed to
recognize and take advantage of the growth opportunities on the other side of life. In other situations, however,
it might hinder the soul's advancement by binding it to
loved ones left behind; and there is also the danger that
getting wrapped up in communication with the dead will
impede a productive life for those still in the material
world. In some instances it is hard to determine whether
extended contact with the deceased helps or hinders.

We can imagine that this uncertainty is faced by
many people who have the opportunity to communicate
with dear souls who have gone on. One woman, whose
husband had passed away two years before, asked Edgar
Cayce whether or not it was advisable to foster ongoing
communication. The counsel she received in her reading
was an endorsement of such effort—with certain quali-
fications. If the communication ''is for a helpful experience to each, it is well. Let it rather be directed by that
communion with Him who has promised to be *with* thee
always . . .'' The woman was then warned not to hinder
her companion, ''but—in such associations and meetings—give the direction to the Holy One.'' (1782-1)

Cayce's answer encourages us to base our decision
as to whether to seek communication with the dead on
an honest evaluation of the effect this interaction is
likely to have on their spiritual development. He is also
saying that in making this judgment we should follow
divine guidance, which he assures us will be available
always.

In some cases our help may be crucial, such as shown
in our next report. Extremely harmful consequences can
result from a person's failure to realize that he or she

has died. In strong contrast with most of our other stories, which describe contact with the deceased as a joyful and reassuring experience, the persistent presence of this woman's husband caused her to become severely depressed. Fortunately, she was able to help him overcome his difficulty, and both of them were able to go on with their lives in their respective spheres.

A NEAR SUICIDE

This account is the continuation of a story told in Chapter 3 by a woman whose husband was killed in battle. Here she tells us of a serious problem that arose after his passing, and the straightforward way in which she solved it.

"Sensing my dead husband's constant presence with me and not being able to see him, speak to him, or comfort him in any way, I felt myself being driven to join him. One night I sat with the pills ready to take my own life.

"Then I thought, 'Maybe he doesn't know that he's dead!' So I spoke out to him, telling him that he had died and that I could not see him or hear him or help him. I told him that there was a place prepared for him to go to, as there was work for him to do there and he was needed. He went!''   *R. S.*

OTHER WAYS OF RELEASING THE DEAD

Praying for the dead and informing them that they have passed on are just two of the steps we can take to assist them in overcoming restrictive bonds to the earth plane. The Cayce readings indicate that proper disposition of their physical remains can also help free the departed from material attachments.

For some individuals the tie between the soul and the body can be powerful enough to keep the soul from leaving the body behind when physical life is over. This can make it necessary, as the Cayce readings put it, to loosen "the elementals from the physical body" so that the soul will be free to move on. (275-29) Some methods of treating the corpse accomplish this "loosening" more completely than do others. The variation depends upon the consciousness of the soul that has passed on.

Two approaches that Cayce mentioned were cremation and hermetically sealing the body in its casket (i.e., "the separation of the atmosphere from the body"). (275-29) Cremation was indicated in several readings; but in my understanding, it is important to wait three full days after physical death before this procedure.

Another important thing we can do to release the dead is simply to avoid becoming a negative influence on their development. Many people would be truly dismayed if they realized how much they were holding back their loved ones by adopting unhelpful attitudes toward their passing. Excessive, possessive grief is particularly harmful in this regard. We must learn to let go of the souls we care about, so that they will be allowed to proceed with their spiritual advancement.

The following story tells of a vivid dream encounter with a soul who was apparently being held to the earth by something unfinished in his relationship with his grown child. Quite possibly this restrictive bond was reenforced by the daughter's sadness and guilt over the circumstances of the parent's death. When the two met and accomplished what had been left undone between them, the problem was resolved and the father was able to move on.

A FATHER'S GOOD-BYE

The contributor of this account beautifully expresses how very dear to us a departed soul can be, and yet how important it is for us to let the soul go. The final paragraph conveys a strong sense of the healing brought about by this release

"I belong to an A.R.E. dream group in Massachusetts, so I keep a journal of my dreams. But in all the years since my father passed on, I have been able to remember very few. My father appeared to me in two of them, and in one we actually touched and talked with each other.

"Some time after my father's death, I dreamed that I was going away on vacation. Just before I left my room, my father suddenly appeared out of nowhere. I said to him, 'I'm going now. Aren't you going to say good-bye to me?'

"But he didn't answer me—he just kept on walking down the hall.

"Two weeks later I had a more intense encounter with my father. In this dream, he and I were living together, and I was younger than I am now. I told him I was going out for a short while to run an errand. He insisted on hugging me before I left. (Even though I loved my father dearly, we had seldom hugged.) He had a very sad look in his eyes, as if he thought something would happen to him before I got back home again. Evidently I went out, and at that point the dream ended.

"These dreams were extremely important to me because my dear father had died very suddenly while he was downtown one day. Before I heard about his collapse, he had been taken to a hospital, and I never saw him alive again. I never got a chance to say good-bye to him and to tell him how much I loved him. This had bothered me for years. I have felt very sad about it and also guilty.

"I believe that when my father hugged me in the second dream we were actually together in bodiless consciousness, for the experience was very vivid, and I sensed I was really with him again. I know now that in these dreams we were finally saying good-bye to each other for the last time because we hadn't gotten the chance to do so while he was still alive. It was a spiritual parting, and since that time I have never had another dream about him.

"I now feel at peace within myself, after all these years. I had to let my father go for his higher spiritual development, and he had to let me go for my spiritual growth on earth. We had both been holding onto each other because of the strong love between us, which continued even beyond the grave. I know that whatever spiritual plane my father is now on he is happy and at peace, and I am sure that we will be together again in another lifetime."   *C. K.*

As this story suggests, the grief of the living can be a severe hindrance to the progress of the departed. It may be natural for us to feel sadness at the passing of a loved one, but we should be careful not to let our mourning become excessive in either intensity or duration. Unrestrained grief can hold a soul to the earth in bonds of sorrow. The result is quite different from the joyful presence the deceased usually display under other circumstances.

Another story—which was told to me many years ago—shows the sharp distinction between the sorrow of souls bound by grief and the happiness of those on the other side who have been granted their release. In most cases the love between parent and child that endures after death is a source of strength and consolation. But, as the father in this story learns, if that love gives rise to excessive sorrow, it can be very harmful to both the living and the deceased. Yet, this is essentially a tale of hope, for it gives us a clear picture of the joy that is available to the departed once our grief over their transition is controlled.

A FATHER'S GRIEF CREATES A BARRIER

A baby girl was born blind to a loving family. There was an especially strong rapport between the child and her father. When the girl was about five years old, she insisted on waiting at the gate every evening for her daddy to come home from work.

Then, to the great dismay of her family, the child became ill and died. The father, in particular, was inconsolable in his grief. His distress interfered with his giving the proper attention to his work, and he lost his job. For two years, weather permitting, he sat in a rocking chair in the yard, thinking about his departed daughter and mourning for her.

One day as the father sat there in sorrow, he had a vision. A great light appeared on the right side of the road. The left side was in semidarkness. On the right side he saw Jesus surrounded by a group of happy, laughing children. On the left he saw his own little girl, all alone in the gloom. Jesus beckoned to her to come over to where He was. But the child, sobbing, said, "I can't as long as my daddy cries for me!"

This experience helped the father become aware of the misery his own anguish was causing his daughter. In the days that followed, he forced himself back to normal. Certainly his pain was greatly eased once he realized the happiness that was awaiting his little girl.

Clearly, in this story the natural remorse that comes with losing a loved one turned into destructive grief. The next report plainly shows the difference between my correspondent's natural sadness over the departure of her father and her mother's extreme, destructive grief. An important part of this account is the explicit plea for help our narrator received from the deceased, a clear expres-

sion of the soul's desire to progress. It seems that sending this message was of some benefit to the departed, as
can be seen in his more peaceful presence at the end of
the story.

THE HARMFULNESS OF
PROLONGED GRIEF

This story was contributed by the same woman who was
visited by her darling nephew Toby after his death—as
told in Chapter 2. Here she gives us an acute sense of
how very detrimental excessive remorse can be to both
the living and the dead.

"My second experience of contact with the deceased
occurred about three months after my father's death.
Daddy died quite unexpectedly—to the family, anyway—
of a heart attack. He and my mother had been married
for thirty-three years. Mother, who had been just fifteen-
and-a-half when they wed, was devastated by his death.

"During the time we were making funeral arrangements, I always felt that Daddy was right by my side.
The sensation was so strong that I felt I could reach out
and touch him. Although I really missed my father, I
never grieved for him, because I was continually aware
of his presence. I also knew that we had been together
before this life and that we would be together again.

"My mother almost destroyed herself with grief. She
spent most of her time either asleep or doped up on
tranquilizers. I always know—I get a feeling—when
things aren't well with her. Mother lives in Louisiana,
and I spent a lot of time going back and forth to visit
her there; but no one could help her pull herself out of
the dark, deep hole she had dug.

"Three months after Daddy died, he came to me during the night. He said, 'Help me, Linda, help me. I can't

move on. Your mother is holding me to the earth.' He repeated this several times. I could feel his presence and hear his voice, but I couldn't see him.

"When I awoke fully the next morning, I called my mother to tell her that Daddy had come to me and to let her know what he had said. She asked if I thought her grief was keeping him from rest, and I had to tell her it was. She said she would try to remember to control herself.

"Since that time I've sensed that Daddy was with me on several occasions, but it's been a more peaceful presence. For a long while after his visit I couldn't 'find' him, and I had the feeling he was resting. His life hadn't been quite what he'd wanted, which caused him some resentment and pessimism, so I think he needed time to rest before moving on." *L. O. C.*

These accounts of the paralyzing effect of grief remind me of a question that was asked at the end of one of my public lectures: "Why do I keep dreaming of my deceased mother wading in water up to her knees?"

I answered, "Ask her!" This woman later reported to me that the next time her mother appeared in one of her dreams, she asked her why she was wading in that water. The mother sorrowfully answered her daughter by saying, "These are the tears you have shed for me. Won't you please let me go?"

The dream awakened the daughter to the suffering she was causing her mother. She then restrained herself, in order to permit her mother to move on, and the disturbing dreams ceased.

THE POWER OF PRAYER

How many of us, when bereft of a loved one, have blamed ourselves for the things we failed to do? "If only I had been more kind to her," we might say. Or, "I wish I had told him more often that I loved him." "I wish I had been more considerate." "I wish I had been more thankful for all she did for me." "I wish . . ."

It may be understandable for us to feel this type of remorse. But such thoughts overlook one vital and extremely comforting truth: death does not end our chance to aid those about whom we care. We can still help them—and help them in some very important ways. But wringing our hands will not do it. Prayer will. Of all the possible difficulties of the deceased that we have seen in the last two chapters, every one of them can be surmounted by the prayers of the living. In prayer we have our best opportunity to continue expressing our love for the people dear to us who have passed on.

Whether our loved ones are living or dead, the best thing we can do for them is to help them draw nearer to God. In one reading, Edgar Cayce described how souls on the other side are attentive to and hope to receive our prayers. This reading assures us that anxiety on behalf of the departed is not needed; through our prayers and the example we set, we can extend to them the strength and guidance needed for their approach to our Creator. In an inspiring image of the receptivity of departed souls, that reading says: "Those who have passed through God's other door are oft listening, listening for the voice of those they have loved in the earth . . . And the prayers of others that are still in the earth may ascend to the throne of God . . ." (3954-1)

Whether souls are in this world or the next, what they ask for will give us a pretty good idea of what it is they value. In stories of contact with the other side, I have never heard of the dead asking anyone for money, or a new car, or nice clothes. But I have heard of a great many instances in which the departed have plainly asked the living for prayer. Each of these cases demonstrates that the deceased want to progress. The souls who request aid know they need help, and they are willing and able to ask for it. Perhaps most significant, they recognize the value of our prayers and their power to give them what they need.

Can we, still living in the physical world, possibly be sure that our prayers do in fact help the dead? Yes, we can—if we listen to them. No one could ask for a clearer expression of the value of prayer than the request I once received.

One evening, a neighbor who knew of my belief in life after death called and asked me to come to her home in order to comfort her husband, who was dying of cancer. The man was weeping constantly because of his fear of death. When I arrived at their home, I tried to soothe him and assure him of the survival of the soul. I pointed out Biblical experiences, particularly those of Jesus and others who had appeared after death. His wife Margaret and I were able to calm him to a degree.

In a few weeks, my neighbor passed on. As is my custom, I prayed for him for about a month; then I ceased. One night about a week later, just as I was awakening, I heard his voice saying, "Please continue to pray for me. I still need your help." Two or three weeks after this incident I again heard his voice. This time he said, "Tell Margaret everything is O.K. now. She has taken care of all the business affairs and other matters perfectly."

When I gave the woman this message, she said, "That fits. I felt him around for weeks. Now that I have finished with all the legal papers, I no longer feel his presence."

I have received other stories that plainly show that our efforts on behalf of the dead are worthwhile. If our prayers were not doing any good, why would the departed bother to keep asking for them? One woman reported frequent dreams of her deceased father—with settings that were almost always in or near a church. She realized this was a symbolic request for prayer. In the following story of another person's dream, the call for prayer is clear and unambiguous:

ANOTHER REQUEST FOR HELP

"One morning I received a phone call from Larry, someone I had worked with at Aberdeen Proving Ground, in Maryland. Larry stated that he had dreamed about Ralph, another man I had known at Aberdeen, who passed away some nine years ago.

"In the dream, Ralph had shown Larry the area of a river where Ralph's boat had sunk. He asked Larry to help him recover it. Larry was able to get the boat off the bottom of the river, but it came to the surface of the water upside down. Larry got up on the vessel and tried to paddle it to land—using his hands, since he had no oars—but he and the boat drifted farther and farther from shore.

"Suddenly in the dream a huge whale appeared. Larry tried to get him to bump the boat to shore. The whale refused to do this but told Larry to get on his back and he would take him in to land. Larry gave up on the boat, jumped on the whale's back, and was brought to shore. Then the dream ended.

"When Larry asked what I thought about this dream, I told him briefly that Ralph apparently is stranded where he is and that he wants to progress but needs help. Since Ralph was a Catholic, I recommended that Larry have Masses said for him and pray for him, and I promised to do the same. I also suggested that Larry himself could be in 'troubled waters' and that he, too, could receive help from Jesus if he would ask. He said he would pray for Ralph and have Masses offered for him.

"Larry has not had any more dreams or messages from Ralph since that time."   *W. J. W.*

I once received a dream message concerning my husband Bill after his death. It showed a similar desire to progress and a need for help. In the dream, Bill was driving around in his truck, carrying his own coffin with him. When I inquired as to the reason for this, he said, "I can't find any place to rest."

This was definitely a call for prayer. According to Edgar Cayce, prayer puts light around the departed souls. This brings them to the attention of helpers on the other side of life, who then rescue them and lead them on to their next stage of development.

Perhaps the need for this kind of assistance in the afterlife is indicated in our next account. Here we meet two souls with a very sad, forlorn quality that suggests they could well require guidance from other beings in the nonphysical realm.

APPEALS FROM TWO SAD GHOSTS

This account tells of two experiences in which the dead do not transmit their requests very explicitly. My correspondent shows great sensitivity to the souls' need for help—and an intuitive understanding of how this assistance can best be given.

"Within a year after the death of a famous singer, I dreamed that he came to visit me in the kitchen where I was cooking. He appeared to be very sad and humble. He did not say anything, but I knew he needed prayers.

"The same thing happened when my stepfather died. I was washing the stone stairs that lead to my home, and he was standing down below, looking up at me. He appeared very forlorn, and I felt he needed help. I invited him into the kitchen. He said nothing—he just looked sad and lost. My family and I knew this was a call to pray for him."   A. F.

Through their requests for prayer, the deceased demonstrate the value they place on this type of aid. Like the living, the dead are capable of showing that they recognize the worth of what they have been given—they can thank us for it. In the previous chapter we saw one incident in which a message of appreciation for prayer was received: the story about Olga Worrell and the souls on my personal prayer list. In a similar fashion I received a report from one person who dreamed of being forbidden to cross a chain-link fence. On "the other side" of this fence was a friend who had passed on—someone for whom my correspondent had been praying. The friend was standing on the far side of the fence and expressing thanks for the prayers.

The deceased are thankful for prayer support because it helps them in very specific ways: to move through the period of unconsciousness that commonly follows death; to assist them in overcoming limiting ties that would bind them to the earth; and even playing a part in the soul's release from "hell" itself. Some of the following accounts are from the many I have received which shows the effect of prayer:

LIFE IN DEATH

In the dream related here, our narrator helps her deceased cousin regain consciousness in the afterlife. Through this vision, my correspondent received a perfectly clear confirmation that her efforts were of real benefit to the departed soul:

"One of my experiences with those who have crossed over involved my cousin Louise. Of all my girl cousins, Louise was the nearest to me in age. We had been especially close in childhood, often playing together. In time she married an airman and moved to England, while I continued my life in Boston.

"Because of our close relationship, it was a terrible shock to me to receive a letter saying that Louise and her new husband had perished in an automobile accident. Remembering from my extensive reading about death that souls often have a struggle to free themselves after an accident or sudden demise, I began praying hard for her. About a week later I had this dream:

"I was in a place of mists, searching for Louise. After a while I found her. She was sleeping, so I shook her to awaken her, calling her name. When she awakened, she kept repeating, 'I'm alive, I'm alive, I'm alive!' I jokingly said, 'Of course, you're alive,' but she was getting almost hysterical. Then others came, and the scene disappeared.

"I remember waking with an even stronger sense than ever before that there is life after death." *S. B. W.*

THE VENGEFUL GHOST

I once learned of a ghost intent upon revenge—a soul who had been wronged and who remained about the earth in an attempt to get even. Prayer and a sincere request for forgiveness were the keys to eliminating this destructive attachment to the physical.

A man whose wife had terminal cancer told me this story. During the prolonged period of her illness, a nurse was present to care for her around the clock. This woman, who was on twenty-four-hour duty, was staying on the second floor of the family home. Several months after she moved in, she began sleeping with the dying woman's husband. Some time later, the wife passed on. The husband then married the nurse.

One day the man called and told me someone was trying to kill his present wife. They lived on the second floor, and their bedroom opened onto a balcony. It was here that the new wife felt the presence of "someone" who was trying to push her over the balcony railing to her death on the pavement below! She said she thought it was her husband's first wife.

I told her that I believed she was right—it was the wife whom she had replaced. I added that the dead woman was probably doing this because of the second wife's activities while she was still alive. I suggested that the new wife pray for the deceased one and that she and her husband both ask her for forgiveness. This they did, and in a very short time there was peace in their home again.

This episode reminded me of many similar stories of haunted houses. These incidents usually happen in places where crimes or sudden death have taken place. Many of the buildings are haunted by deceased persons who do not know that they have died. This makes prayer for the dead most important, for it allows them to be helped by beings on the other side whose duty it is to direct these "lost souls."

Our next story concerns another resentful ghost. Two factors—prayer plus the communication of a desire for forgiveness—are the means used to overcome the ill feelings of the deceased. The report closes with an indication of a gradual improvement in the situation, which parallels what we might expect to find happening in an association between two living people. Restoring harmony in a relationship can take time and sustained effort, whichever side of life the person we are seeking reconciliation with is to be found.

ANOTHER UNFORGIVING SOUL

In this account we can again see the way in which negative emotions hinder the development of the departed soul and disturb the peace of the living. This story shows grounds for hope that the resentment of the deceased will in time be healed, due largely to our narrator's determination to mend the relationship.

*   *   *

"For many months I have had a series of dreams about Earl. The dreams, which are always the same, give me a feeling of 'now'—even though Earl is no longer in this dimension.

"The dream occurs amid crowded activity, with many people milling about. It appears I am constantly trying to greet Earl. But even though he sees me, he turns and walks away, ignoring my overtures. His shoulders are hunched and he resolutely walks off in another direction.

"The other night, in my dream, I actually caught hold of Earl's hand; but he threw my hand away with an angry gesture. He then turned his back to me and stood there stiff and hostile.

"Obviously, for some reason Earl is angry with me, and he remains upset even though he has passed on. All I can do is pray for him and send him the message that I am sorry for having, in some way, offended him. I pray that he will forgive and forget, so that we may both continue peacefully on in our lives—I in this dimension and he over there.

"The last dream experience I had with Earl showed me a softening of his attitude. This time he did not walk away. He merely turned his back, which suggests some improvement in his feelings toward me."   *S. M.*

A final story illustrates the power of *group* prayer, which can release a surprising amount of physical energy. More important, it can even reach into "hell" and free someone in outer darkness.

One night I attended a meeting of a prayer and meditation group to which I belonged. At the close of every group meeting we always prayed for the ill, the troubled, the dying, and the dead. As part of this prayer we always remembered "those souls who have passed on and are in outer darkness."

On this particular night, in the silence that followed our mention of the souls in outer darkness, there was a flash of light, and we all experienced the distinct odor of ozone. After the prayer period, we discussed the experience and concluded that someone somewhere had been reached and helped.

Soon after I was in bed, thinking about the incident. Suddenly I was aware of a visitor! A bald-headed Oriental, well dressed, was coming out of a great darkness, head bowed, moaning to himself and saying, "It's too late, too late to save me!"

I immediately gathered that this was the soul who had been touched by the group's prayers that evening. I tried to assure him that it was never too late to turn to God and be helped. That night, the prayer of our group had indeed reached a soul in outer darkness.

11

GLIMPSES OF THE WORLD BEYOND

IN THIS FINAL chapter, we look at some of the most fascinating and inspiring of the accounts I have received. They are a fitting conclusion to our collection—some of the strongest evidence imaginable to support the principle that life is continuous. Some of these stories concern healing or out-of-body experiences; others, remarkable encounters with the Christ; and still others, convincing descriptions of what life may be like once we shed the physical body.

The first story is a lengthy account of personal healing and transformation. It is the longest report I have included in this book, and it beautifully describes the sincere search of one soul to find a deeper meaning to her life.

A SPIRITUAL AWAKENING

In this story our narrator shares with us a number of special events that she experienced. Taken together, these occurrences suggest that there are worlds beyond our own and a life beyond the physical.

"In January of 1977, I asked if there was such a thing as survival of death. Like most people, I didn't really believe there was. But I thought that if there was, our existence after death would be more pleasant than physical life; and if there was only oblivion, that, too, would be better than this. So, either way, death would be preferable. I wasn't asking my questions of anyone in particular. I didn't know anyone to ask. The morning after considering these thoughts I awoke, turned over onto my left side, and relaxed.

"Suddenly I found myself out-of-my-body, moving through space. I stopped at a place where, as I discovered later, the Akashic Records were kept. A man was waiting there for me. He read to me from the left- and right-hand pages of what appeared to be a rather large, golden-colored book.

"When he had finished, I walked along a pathway until I came to an arched opening. I passed through it into a very large reception room, where there was only an urn with a dried branch in it and a man dressed in a white, floor-length robe with a cowl around his face.

"I was looking at the branch in the urn and thinking, 'Wouldn't that make a beautiful gardenia bush?' As I thought this, leaves began to appear on it, and a gardenia grew at the top of the side closest to me.

"I looked at the man standing there, and he conveyed telepathically, 'Welcome to this place.' I truly have never felt more welcome anywhere. As he said this, other figures began to join us from my right. All were dressed the same way, except for four or five who wore golden robes instead of white. They, too, were thinking, 'Welcome.'

"Then the first one said, 'We know you grow weary in the earth.' And I knew they did know. Everyone there understood each thought as it was being formed—even I. Then the man said, 'When you grow weary, think of the white gardenia and remember.'

"I said, 'But the gardenia will be gone tomorrow.'

"He replied, 'Yes, it will. But it will be there when you choose to remember it. So remember, and you may rest here between times.'

"Then I returned to earth. I had looked at the bedside

clock before I turned over onto my left side, so I know thirty minutes had passed. It took me ten minutes to reach that other world, I stayed ten minutes, and it took me ten minutes to get back. However, while I was over there, it seemed that many, many years were passing on earth. Everything in that world was ethereal, and there were only two colors—white and gold. That afternoon I asked my husband Paul about my experience, and he said it was probably a dream; but I insisted it was not a dream.

"A few days later, while browsing in a book exchange, I walked by a shelf labeled 'Occult.' As I didn't know that word, I stopped to see what kind of books were there. I selected two about Edgar Cayce: *Venture Inward* and *The Edgar Cayce Reader #2*. I had visited an Association for Research and Enlightenment study group one night in Midland, Texas, about fifteen years ago, but it did not leave a lasting impression on me.

"The Saturday after I picked up those two books, I lay down on the couch and happened to open *Venture Inward*. There, in a description of what Edgar Cayce experienced while giving a reading, I found, 'I see myself as a tiny dot out of my physical body . . .' Even though this was not exactly the same experience as mine, I was excited. I jumped up and ran to Paul, saying, 'See, someone else has done that, too! I told you it was real and not a dream.' He said nothing.

"After reading the two books I decided to try meditation. I lay down, face up, and closed my eyes. A tremendously bright light appeared, even though my eyes were closed. I was so frightened I quickly opened my eyes, and the light disappeared. The next night in bed I tried it again, and the same thing happened; and again on the third night.

"The fourth night I told myself, 'I am going to hold it this time, just so I can see what will happen.' When the light appeared, I tried asking some questions. My first one was 'Is reincarnation a fact?' The answer I received was 'Yes. It is a gift from God.' While thinking this over, I fell asleep.

"The next night I tried meditating once more, with my eyes closed. The light appeared again, so I opened my eyes to look around the room. When I did so, I saw a whirling circle come toward me. It seemed to enter my head. I was blind for two-and-one-half hours and fearful I might never see again!

"The following night I had breathing difficulties and felt miserable. My discomfort lasted for three days and two nights, during which time I could neither eat, drink, nor smoke a cigarette. Finally, on the third night, I was sitting up in the middle of my bed thinking, 'I must have been mistaken. What a fool I was to have thought there is anything more than this life. Everything else is only in my imagination. Paul was right. I am going out of my mind; there's no one to help me.' I talked myself into being totally without hope again.

"At that moment I glanced at the wall in front of me and seemed to be looking past a rather large, white building with tall columns. It reminded me of a Greek temple. There were a lot of trees growing in front of it, and it was half-covered with vines and many beautiful flowers. I also found myself looking beyond the profiles of golden-headed people. Thirteen figures, all dressed differently, appeared. Among them were a Japanese man in costume, a robed Tibetan, and a Chinese man wearing a dress of gold and a little round hat studded with many jewels. I watched the Chinese person for a long time.

"Then I noticed a barefooted man. He was dressed in a woven garment with holes for the head and arms. He was the most beautiful figure of a man I have ever seen: muscular, with wonderful features, auburn hair, and blue eyes. As I looked into those eyes, I knew who he was—Jesus of Nazareth! No words can describe what I felt at that moment! As I gazed at Him, He let me

know how to get rid of the negative vibrations I had
been feeling.''   *B. J. N.*

This report tells of several interesting and unusual happenings. Two of these incidents are of types that we'll
be looking at in this chapter. The woman's first experience was a voyage out-of-body. This journey took her
to another world, far different from the material one she
found so tiresome. The beauty and peacefulness of this
realm is quite similar to those visited by a number of
my other correspondents. In their stories, as here, strong
evidence suggests that the physical dimension which is
home to our bodies is just one of many domains in
which we can reside.

Later, after beginning the practice of meditation, our
narrator had a healing encounter with Jesus. Like several
of my other sources who have described meetings with
special beings, this woman's experience occurred at a
time when it was greatly needed—a time of depression
that was ''totally without hope.'' Then, through her
meeting with the Master, her spirits were uplifted and
she was shown how to overcome her negative feelings.
Jesus' effectiveness as guide and healer, demonstrated
here and in the next few stories, shows that He truly is
alive.

Many souls have had the experience of meeting Jesus
in visions and dreams. These encounters demonstrate
that He is active on all planes of consciousness. His
promise, ''I will be with you always'' (Matthew 28:20),
was meant for all people who are trying to live by the
laws given in the Ten Commandments. This pledge assures us of the reality of His continuing presence. It is
His word to us that physical death is not the end—that
our experiences with others who have moved on can be
valid. Just as surely, it is a promise of this guidance and
protection while we are still here in materiality. For example, in a vision, Edgar Cayce once saw Jesus—who
was a figure of central importance throughout his life—

giving a personal message to each individual gathered in a study group. The face of the Master changed as He communicated with each member present. The purpose of this vision was to reassure Cayce that the source of his information was reliable and all was well.

JESUS, THE FAITHFUL HEALER

In other material I have gathered, Jesus appears as a healer. The effective cures brought about during these encounters provide convincing evidence that the touch of the Master has truly been felt. As might be expected, these events can have a very strong impact upon the people involved in them.

I personally have seen the results of one such healing. As the person who received this cure was telling me of his experience, I was struck by the vivid feeling he communicated of having been in Jesus' immediate presence.

Though I didn't actually witness the vision described in this story, I did see its astonishing effect. This incident shows that Jesus' love and ability to help us are more than just a nice-sounding theory; they can be a very real force in our lives.

Some time ago I was in Dallas, Texas, on a lecture tour with Edgar Cayce's son, Hugh Lynn. While we were there, Hugh Lynn became very ill. His temperature rose above 104 degrees. I had taken over his responsibilities for the evening, but I was concerned about our continuing the trip the next day.

The Dallas study group of the A.R.E. gathered that evening for a social, at the end of which we were all asked to join in a closing meditation. The meditation period lasted for perhaps fifteen or twenty minutes, after which the group prepared to leave. At that point Hugh Lynn, who had gotten dressed just in order to take part in the meditation, jumped up and began to tie books together, pack them away, and prepare for the continuation of our tour.

I was shocked to see Hugh Lynn, whom I believed to be very ill, working so hard when I felt he should be in bed, resting for the next day's trip. I therefore spoke to him, suggesting that he go back to bed and recover his strength for the tasks ahead. He just looked up at me, grinned, and kept on working. Frustrated, I thought to myself, "Men—they're so hard-headed!"

A few days later Hugh Lynn said to me, "I think I owe you an explanation." He then proceeded to tell me that during the final evening's meditation meeting in Dallas he had suddenly become aware of a brilliant light in the room, which caused him to open his eyes to discover its origin. To his great surprise, he saw Jesus standing in the center of the room smiling at him! Needless to say, Hugh Lynn was astounded.

The Master spoke to him, saying, "Why are you so surprised? You are always telling people I can come to them. Well, I'm here to heal you!"

And Hugh Lynn was healed at that moment.

Another story of Jesus as healer came my way and made an impression on me. It has several features I have mentioned earlier. In it we find the strength and encouragement the living can derive from contact with a departed loved one. We see another soul—an earthbound one—and the harmful influence such a being can exert. And we recognize once again that this problem can be overcome through prayer and compassionate communication—particularly if one enlists the aid of a loving and powerful Friend.

CHRIST'S LOVE EXEMPLIFIED

This moving account demonstrates Jesus' love for us and His ability to bring peace and healing into our lives. The change that came about in our narrator's husband shows that her vision of the Master was indeed valid.

"When my father-in-law died about ten years ago, my mother-in-law became very despondent. Although perfectly well physically, she was unable to cope on her own. She wanted to lean on my husband, her eldest son. But unfortunately we lived in the United States and she lived in England. We visited her across the ocean and did what we could for her, but obviously we were limited by the distance. She continued to refuse to make an effort to stand on her own feet, and as time went by my husband became depressed and started to drink heavily.

"My mother-in-law resented me because she blamed me for our being in the United States. She kept telling me that I could force my husband to return to England if I so wanted. Her condemnation of me was completely unwarranted; but, since she believed it to be justified, she started to attack me verbally and criticize me to other family members, including my husband. I suppose she felt that all her problems would be solved if we moved to England and 'looked after' her, as she put it.

"During this difficult period, my deceased father-in-law, who had been very close to me, visited me several times. It seemed that he came when things were at their worst, as if to reassure me that he understood. I would sense his presence in the room, usually when it was quiet and I was alone. He always appeared loving and approving.

"Finally, about nine years after his death, my mother-in-law also passed away. My husband, who had been drinking all this time, began to get worse. He plunged deeper into alcoholism, and he even feigned heart attacks and made suicide threats. At the same time he seemed to take on some of his mother's worst traits. After a few months we discovered that he had a liver disease and would have to stop drinking. But at first he refused; he seemed incapable of understanding his danger. This was totally uncharacteristic of him, since he is a very intelligent man.

"At that point I decided to do some serious praying. I sensed that my mother-in-law was still earthbound and exerting a negative influence on both of us. I truly felt we were fighting for my husband's life—that if she could, she would take him with her!

"After asking for some time how best to pray, I saw a picture of Christ on the cross, taking my husband's alcoholism on Himself. The whiskey bottles and beer cans were piled at the foot of the cross. Then I saw Jesus walking away from the cross with His arm around my husband, talking to him lovingly. I was reminded of the words of the Bible: ' . . . with his stripes we are healed.' (Isaiah 53:5) The vision filled me with a peace I had not known since my father-in-law's death.

"I then began to pray in Jesus' name for my mother-in-law to leave my husband alone and continue on her journey in the afterlife without him. At first, as I prayed for her, I felt a wall of antagonism. After a while, I sat down and 'talked' with her whenever I felt her presence, telling her that she must get on with her life, that her son's life on earth was not finished, and that she had no right to expect him to go with her. I also told her that if she looked carefully she would find people waiting to help her, and that she would be blessed and protected as she continued on her way. While holding these 'conversations,' I surrounded her with as much love as I was capable of. Finally, during my third attempt to reach her, I saw her husband Sam come for her. They turned and left together.

"That very week my husband stopped drinking. He realized his plight with alcohol, a problem which he told me he had not understood before now, because his vision had been clouded. He has been a completely different person since—young at heart again, like the man I married. This change is truly remarkable, especially when you consider that the average Alcoholics Anonymous member is not healed spiritually until two or three years after the drinking has been stopped.''

S. H.

CONTACT WITH OTHER SPECIAL BEINGS

Both my own experiences and the material I have received show that communication is possible with special benevolent beings in addition to Jesus. In a sense, this could apply to all helpful contact with the departed, such as my correspondent reported with her father-in-law in the above story. There are other cases, however, in which it seems that help is received, not from the recently dead, but from some other source.

Many of us believe that every individual has one or more guardian angels. Numerous people have reported hearing a voice or seeing a sign that protected them from danger. Edgar Cayce was certainly among those who received on many occasions various warnings from beyond the physical realm.

I, too, have been shielded from harm in this way. A voice that was without any physical source kept my husband and me from arriving in Beirut, Lebanon, the day war broke out. A vivid dream saved friends of mine from possible death. Another dream which featured red and green traffic lights probably saved my own life. On another occasion a voice warned me against taking a certain medicine, and also said, ''Do not go swimming today.'' But when I disobeyed this advice, the result was a case of pneumonia. Intervention by such other-worldly agents—''guardian angels'' perhaps—shows that we have more help available to us than we are commonly aware of, and that the distance between the physical and the spiritual realms is not as great as we might think.

This closeness between the two worlds is apparent in

our next story, in which we meet beings from beyond the physical. Here we can see that contact of this sort does not always occur in order to protect us from danger. In this instance it seems that the presence of my correspondent's "supernatural" visitors may well have uplifted her spirits and helped her move through a time of sorrow.

AN ANGELIC DAUGHTER'S DEPARTURE

In this account it seems that supernatural beings outside our narrator's window strengthened her sense that her daughter was a special soul. In this feeling the woman may have found consolation and an understanding of the purpose of her child's brief life.

"At only five months of age, my daughter died in 1970. A few days later, through my bedroom window I saw— or psychically felt—creatures similar to ghosts. These visitors stayed for about a month, always sitting outside the same window. I had no idea why they came, what they were doing, or what exactly they were, because up to that time I had been unaware of any supernatural beings whatever.

"Today I would have to say they could best be described as either a host of ghosts or a host of angels. In my opinion they were the latter. I feel my daughter was close to having been an angel herself. To me she was perfect, and I believe she came into my life to awaken me and to set me on a new path.

"The day my baby died, my four-year-old son was playing with his toy telephone. Suddenly he said, 'Mom, Julie's calling from heaven and wants to talk to you.' I have wondered for years if he wasn't right!''   *V. B.*

*   *   *

Our next account is another in which we are told of contact from beyond the physical world. Though we cannot be sure of the exact nature of the source of this message, the experience shows that beings without material bodies do exist and that they are aware of us and able to communicate with us. Perhaps the point of this story is that our "guardian angels" can offer us comfort as well as guidance and protection.

REASSURANCE FROM BEYOND THE PHYSICAL

As this report shows, it can be a bit disconcerting to receive a message in the way that our contributor did. Nevertheless, we can well imagine that once she got over her initial surprise, the reassuring content of the communication would have greatly eased her mind concerning her daughter.

"In 1976 my husband, my son, and I were living on our mini-farm in Oregon. One day while I was transplanting onions, my mind turned seriously to my daughter, who had just been to visit us from San Francisco a few weeks before.

"I was thinking, 'How could she have been my daughter for seventeen years and not have learned one single thing from me? Were all those years wasted? How is it possible that she learned absolutely nothing from me?'

"A voice said, not with sound but with thought, 'She has learned from you. It may not be obvious to you now, but what you have taught her will always be with her, and she can draw upon it whenever she chooses to do so.'

"I was thinking, 'Well, I certainly hope so,' when it dawned on me that no one else was there. I started look-

ing around to see who was talking and decided that
worry had finally driven me crazy!"   *B. J. N.*

Edgar Cayce had contact with special beings on several
occasions. For example, in a dream he saw himself talking with Jude, the disciple of Jesus. According to the
readings, Jude was not only a disciple of Jesus, he was
also a member of His immediate family—the younger
son of Mary and Joseph. Whether or not this dream conversation was an actual meeting between Cayce and the
soul who had been Jude, it does illustrate the type of
information that can be available to those who are able
to reach beyond the bounds of a single physical lifetime.

In Cayce's unusual dream, Jude appeared as a youthful man, interested in the teachings of the apostles. Jude
told Cayce how he had been very young when Joseph,
his father, had died. He talked about Jesus' return from
Persia to take care of the property and to look after Mary
and the rest of the children.

Jude then described some of the other disciples—Bar-
tholomew, John, Judas, and James. He discussed the last
evening in the garden, the activities of Judas, and his
own ministry during the latter part of his life. He added
that in time Peter's wife and mother-in-law became lead-
ers of the group of women who followed the Master.

EXPERIENCES OUTSIDE THE PHYSICAL BODY

A number of my sources have reported another kind of
special experience which involves the soul leaving the
body. The accounts of these out-of-body adventures
share a striking quality of reality. Some of these stories
tell of people who left the body as they were very close
to dying, but who later recovered. In other cases, the
individuals do *not* seem to have been near death when

they traveled out of their bodies. Both types of experiences give us fascinating glimpses into other worlds and show that there is more to us than just the material part of our being.

Our next two reports tell of out-of-body voyages by people who were not approaching physical death. In the first case, there is no obvious cause for our contributor's experience. The incident described in the second account was evidently brought about by my correspondent's involvement in a parent's transition.

A JOURNEY OUT-OF-THE-BODY

This story tells us of an out-of-body trip that was completely unexpected. We can imagine how great a shock the experience must have been to our narrator, and the reported feeling of fear is certainly understandable. As we shall see from the accounts that follow, both the suddenness of the incident and the accompanying fear are unusual features.

"While making my bed one day late in the summer of 1967 or '68, I suddenly found that I was out of my body. I was floating in a void, with no sense of up or down nor right or left. I felt weightless, and I was frightened that I wouldn't be able to get back to my body.

"As soon as I became aware of this fear, I saw my body—a pink blob far, far away. I willed myself toward it, and the next thing I knew I was back in it, sitting on the bed. I have thought a lot about this experience but have never come up with a reasonable explanation."

K. B.

The next story takes us to what seems to be a border station for souls who are just in the process of making the transition. The account provides a wealth of persuasive evidence that contact with the dying actually took place: the timing of my correspondent's mother's death, the father's coinciding visit from his wife, and the identification of the body in the funeral home.

"My mother was very ill for a long time. Since my parents had been unusually close, my father found it extremely difficult to be at her bedside. Watching her die so slowly took its toll on him, but my mother wasn't able to understand this. When she went into a coma, the doctor rushed her to the hospital, saying she would survive only a day or so. But for the next three weeks members of the family took turns staying with her.

"One night, as in a dream, I seemed to be standing in a place similar to the waiting room of the Kansas City Union Station. It was a huge, high-ceilinged building. I was wearing a coat that had been one of my favorites, purchased shortly after my graduation from college.

"Many people were walking through the area, in one direction only, from my left to my right. There was no visiting of any kind, nor did they notice me. The only furniture was a chair that faced me. It was of a kitchen variety, with the back curving from one side to the other, held together by spokes of different lengths.

"As I waited, I happened to notice a man who walked briskly nearby. He was athletic, blond, and handsome, probably in his fifties.

"Then I saw Mother. She was dressed in her best coat and hat of many years ago. She could scarcely walk. She strained every muscle in her effort to reach me. Then, holding onto the chair, she said, 'My wound never healed on the inside.' With that she collapsed onto the chair, striking its back, which caused her hat to fall off. At this point my visionary experience ended.

"I was completely baffled by what I had seen. At the same time, I became aware of someone crying in the distance. Gradually the sound grew louder. I knew I had to go investigate its source. But when I first tried to move my body, nothing happened. I had great difficulty getting it to respond. Finally I 'came to,' stood up, and made it to the door of the bedroom and on into the dining room.

"There at the table sat my father, crying. Through his tears he looked up and sobbed, 'Mother just told me good-bye.' I could say nothing more than 'Oh?' Then I wilted into a chair across from him. Tearfully, in broken sentences, he recounted how she had come to him and informed him of her death.

"After a long silence I said, 'I saw Mother, too.' My father quickly looked up, inquiringly, and stopped crying. I told him what I had seen and what Mother had said. He drank in every word, seeming to understand.

"We didn't say anything after that. We just waited, knowing that Mother had died and that my sister-in-law, who was at the hospital, would call soon. In about an hour, maybe longer, the expected call came through.

"But the story of this out-of-body experience doesn't really end there. When I went to see Mother after her demise, there was no one at the door of the funeral home to greet me, so I signed the visitors' book and waited. After a while, since there was still no one there, I simply stepped into the first room.

"Suddenly I became speechless, stunned, frozen to the spot. Whom do you think I saw in the casket? It was the same blond-haired fellow who had passed me while I was waiting for Mother! I don't know how long I stood there before I became aware of someone tugging at my arm and taking me into the right room."   *C. P.*

Are humans the only life form that can have an out-of-body experience? Perhaps not. Our next story is interesting in that it suggests that we humans are not the only earthly creatures who have nonphysical elements in our make-up. Apparently animals, too, can at times transcend the limits of the body. The subject of this account was unable to say how her experiences outside the physical might relate to our own. But, as my correspondent's

statements in the last paragraph clearly show, a beloved
pet's return from the other side can bolster our faith in
survival after death, much as would a visit from a deceased human loved one.

A WELL-TRAVELED TERRIER

This story gives us a very engaging picture of the relationship between our narrator and her pet. For those of
us with nonhuman friends, this report suggests the encouraging thought that they, like us, will survive the
passing of the physical.

"Our Boston terrier left us one morning in December
of 1983. I had had a very strong rapport with this small
creature. I even caught her in an out-of-body trip one
evening when she was sleeping near my feet. Her smoky
shape arose from her body and disappeared for a short
while, and then I saw it returning. I spoke to her and
said, 'Hey, Snooks, where have you been?' She raised
her head and looked at me as if to say, 'None of your
business!'

"I have used mental telepathy on her extensively, and
she has always responded, even when I was on the first
floor and she was asleep on the loveseat upstairs. She
would trot down the stairs, come over to me, and look
up with an expression that said, 'You called me?'

"She has also returned to us since her death. We have
seen her playing with her favorite toy, a big red ball,
juggling it just as she did when in her physical body.

"All these experiences have helped my husband and
me to reconfirm our belief that death, as the word is
commonly used, is not the end. We are convinced that
we are, as of this day, the sum total of all our experiences, good and bad; and what we do with these lessons
is entirely up to us, for good or ill. We grow at the pace
we set for ourselves, and our souls retain the essence
that is us. From time to time we may recognize other

souls with whom we have associated in the past and whom we will meet again in the future.''   *D. T.*

NEAR-DEATH EXPERIENCES

In recent years considerable publicity has been given to near-death experiences. In many of these reports it is medical technology that brings a person's physical body back to life after seconds or minutes of being clinically dead. In those moments the soul may get a vivid glimpse of the afterlife. The following stories depict some examples of people who have actually been close to death. These near-death experiences are of particular interest because they may give us an idea of what is waiting for each one of us in the afterlife. Those who take these voyages beyond the physical receive the clearest conceivable demonstration that we can survive independent of the material body. We can imagine that having such an experience would greatly reduce any fear of death a person might have felt previously. In fact, in several of these reports my correspondents state or imply that they did not want to return to the physical once they had seen the other side of life. This reluctance to come back is a striking feature in both of our next two accounts.

A CHILD'S NEAR-DEATH EXPERIENCE

Though the contributor of this story had her close encounter with death at a very young age, it does not seem that the experience frightened her. On the contrary, the strongest feeling her report carries is the sense of freedom she discovered in release from the body.

''When I was just a tiny child—two years, eight months old—I was in an automobile accident that took the lives of both my parents. I myself was not expected to live. I vividly remember 'flying' about my hospital room and seeing my body in the bed below; in fact, this memory is the earliest clear recollection that I have.

"Of course, I did recover. And for many years my story was considered to be just a child's fantasy or a dream. Then came the public discussions of near-death experiences. Now the people around me have decided I was right—it really did happen!"   *C. P. P.*

HAPPINESS AFTER DEATH

I received this story from the same source as the previous one. From the reaction of our out-of-body traveler, we can guess that the world he visited was a realm of great beauty and joy. We might even get the feeling that during the final period of his life he was actually eager for the chance to return there permanently.

"Gram's brother, Bill—my great-uncle—died about two years before she did. At one point during the long illness from which he eventually died, he was declared dead but later revived. To the end of his life he remained thoroughly disgusted with the doctors who had brought him back. He had been having a wonderful time in 'Glory,' he declared. Why did they have to 'drag him back'? Those were his very words.

"I must say that I could sympathize with him. I was furious when they brought me back, too—at the age of two-and-one-half!"   *C. P. P.*

The "Glory" mentioned in this story suggests a domain similar to the one of beauty, peace, and light that was visited by my next correspondent. An important feature of this account is the way in which this woman's trip to another world influenced her. Like several of the people whose stories follow later in this chapter, she was left with an increased desire to do God's will in life. Effects such as this give us good reason to believe that the experiences awaiting all of us at the end of life will be an important and very beneficial part of our journey back to our Creator.

THE LIGHT OF THE WORLD

Quite possibly, this woman's experience was brought about by an intense desire for her physical life to end so that she would be released from pain. Here we have another picture of a world so captivating that our narrator did not want to leave it and return to familiar, material life.

"When I was giving birth to my third child, on October 18, 1946, the pain was enough to warrant my asking God to take me out of this world. I don't remember how I got there, but suddenly I knew I was in a heavenly place. There were countless people, all dressed in white, facing a beautiful white light. Although not a word was said, I knew they were learning from the light. I believed it was God teaching them.

"I tried to join them, but a tall figure in white gently led me aside to gaze down at the earth. I could sense all the turmoil and confusion in the world, and I didn't want to go back—it was so beautiful and peaceful where I was. Without speaking, the figure told me that I must return to my body, for there was much work I was required to do before I could come back to their world.

"As I came out of the anesthetic, I heard someone say, 'Phew! I thought we lost her.' I was still unconscious at that point, and I didn't wake up until an hour later.

"I wish others could have an experience something like mine, as we all have to know that we are here to do God's will on earth."   *F. A. B.*

*   *   *

Our next story is quite unusual in that the nonearthly
world it tells us about appeared to be uninhabited. Perhaps there was no one to greet the woman who made
this journey because she arrived unexpectedly—it was
not yet her time to die. If so, this suggests that death is
not random, that it occurs only when the time is right.

VOYAGE TO A WORLD OF
SOLITUDE

This account takes us to a place somewhat different from
the glorious realms of our last two reports. The flowered
world visited by my correspondent's mother could well
be beautiful; and yet, the predominant feeling it imparted
was one of loneliness.

"On July 25, 1953, my parents and I were in a terrible
automobile accident in the vicinity of Lawrence, Kansas.
My father's shoulder was broken and my mother's spinal
cord was severed. I had only minor injuries and was
released from the hospital after three days. I returned to
our home in Saint Louis, while my parents were kept at
the hospital in Kansas.

"About ten days later, the doctor called and told me
my mother was dying and I should come to see her at
once. I left by bus for Kansas immediately and arrived
at the hospital the next morning. When I got there, the
doctor informed me that Mother had suddenly improved
during the night and apparently would not die. My
mother was not told that she had almost passed away
that night.

"Several months later, when she was back at home
in Saint Louis, Mother told me of an unusual experience
she had had the night before I visited her. She felt herself
leaving her body and walking off down a path bordered

on both sides by exotic flowers. She was all alone, and as she moved along she looked away from the flower-lined path, and she could see the earth rotating below her. She felt lonely and wondered why no one came to meet her. Suddenly there was a loud explosion in front of her, so she turned around and walked back. I suppose this was the point at which she began improving physically.

"Remember that all this happened in 1953, before written reports of the experiences of the clinically dead were generally available to the public. So it wasn't that Mother was just dreaming of something she had read about."   *H. G.*

The narrator of our next story was given the unusual option of returning to physical life or remaining in the spirit realm. Unlike what we might have expected from the participants in several of our foregoing accounts, he chose to come back to the material world. Evidently this man's choice was determined by his strong sense of purpose regarding the proper upbringing of his children. The experience recounted here left him with an increased dedication to this goal.

RESPONSIBILITY GUIDES A CHOICE

This report was contributed by a man whose adventure out-of-body was triggered by a medical emergency. In this interesting description of an experience that took place partly in our own world, partly in another, we can see once again that the physical and spiritual dimensions are closer to each other than we generally realize.

"I heard a buzz and suddenly found myself four feet above my body, observing the hospital staff trying to resuscitate me. A pediatric doctor, who had been first on the scene, was using electric shock in an effort to restart my heart.

"In addition to being able to hear the doctors speak, I was aware of their feelings. The resident physician, whom I knew well, was emotionally upset, and I would describe his feeling as 'love.' This differed from the attitude of the new cardiologist, who felt that he was 'losing the ball game'!

"The staff zapped me twice with the electric device, and at once I was in the waiting room, listening to my wife and mother talk. Then I was contacted telepathically by a being of light, who told me it would be O.K. for me to stay in heaven but also gave me the option of returning to earth. At that point I had the sensation of moving through a tunnel with a light at the end of it. I returned to my body with a renewed determination to raise my five children."   *R. M.*

THE EFFECTS OF EXPERIENCES OUTSIDE THE BODY

The previous account has a feature common in our reports of people who have left the physical body for a time: these individuals frequently return to the material world with increased dedication to what they see as the purpose of their lives. This suggests a reason for these occurrences. These experiences are meant to *change* the people who undergo them, and it seems that in fact they do. The stories I have received give a sense that journeys out-of-body have a powerful impact on those who take them.

The three experiences that follow are similar in their descriptions of positive change, and they have several other elements in common. In each account we are told of a voyage to a world of peace, beauty, and joy—feelings much like those that the living are often left with after a visit from a departed loved one. Each of these accounts also describes an extraordinary growth in consciousness. Here my correspondents have quite possibly received a foretaste of an exciting change awaiting all of us on the other side of life.

One additional feature worth mentioning is the feeling that our language simply cannot convey the quality of these experiences. As one of my sources phrases it, "I can't put into writing the blissful state I was in." And, from another report: "There is so much I cannot write, for words fail me when I try to express His love." Though these individuals may be unable to express fully the aftereffects of their activities outside the physical, it is obvious that each returned to the body different from the person he or she had been before.

A BEAUTIFUL CHRISTMAS EXPERIENCE

The experience described here awakened my correspondent to a new world, a blissful one of peace and fellowship. Perhaps the most important point is that the lifelong impact of this visit stayed with our traveler upon returning to the physical dimension, bringing forth joy, gratitude, and love.

"On Christmas Eve night, I had one of those wonderful experiences which I wish would occur more often. Even just one such incident is a true delight to the heart and leaves it sweetened for a lifetime.

"I was one of hundreds and hundreds of people crossing over to 'the other side.' We were all there for Christ's birthday. It seemed we could not come alone; each of us had to bring a friend. With me was Dottie, my one true soul friend.

"We were pouring into this new world, hands on each other's shoulders, all chanting 'A-um' over and over again. Tears of joy came to my eyes just from seeing this wonderful sight. We came from all walks of life, from all countries and all religions. It was a picture of what I would call pure fellowship; that is, all petty concerns were put aside for the greater good of the world.

"We all sat together. Then one by one, we got up to give our Christmas gift to the Christ, the only gift He truly desires—ourselves. Each of us told what we were doing to help the world in its spiritual evolution. Although there were many hundreds of us, each person rose individually to present his or her gift. Everyone clapped in encouragement for those who stood up. When it was my turn to speak, I said that I had been working hard on improving myself through group activities, prayer and meditation, so that when the time came for me to give to the world I would be prepared. I received a great deal of encouragement for this.

"I was then given a delightful little man as my Christmas present. In his time he had been a world traveler, and he had come to take me on an out-of-body journey around the world. This was something I had always wanted. We ended up in France, where we entered a white pavilion. My guide told me to think of ice-cream sodas, and when I did they manifested before us.

"He then reached across and took my hand. When he let go, he left a medal in my palm. I looked at it and asked, 'What does it do?'

"He just laughed and said, 'We've been waiting for you to wake up.' I said, 'I've been waiting for that myself!'

"I woke from this sleep on Christmas morning. I can't put into writing the blissful state I was in. I wanted to get down on my knees and kiss the earth in gratitude for its being. Everything around me was in brilliant color, and my love for my family and friends seemed to know no bounds. Life was a treasure from the great treasure-house of God!

"As I meditated that night, my mind opened up like a delicate flower and I sat viewing the stars and the universe in all their glory. I don't know how it was possible for me to see the universe and the stars inside my head, but that's what I experienced.

"This had been the best Christmas and, by far, the best Christmas present of my entire life. I shall never forget it. What rapture!"   *J. M. B.*

In our next story we are not given as many particulars about the world that was visited. But the description of how this adventure affected my correspondent is quite detailed. While outside the body, our traveler experienced a vastly expanded consciousness and a feeling of timelessness. Also of interest is the mention of gender-free existence—a state of being in which male and female qualities are combined. This is a condition hinted at in the Edgar Cayce readings. Again, this journey out-of-body produced a vital element: an increased compassion, which arose from the growth in our narrator's awareness.

INTO A TIMELESS WORLD

The experience related here had a profound effect on our contributor that apparently has lasted long after the voyage beyond the physical itself was over. If the non-material realm my correspondent describes is a true indication of what waits for us in the afterlife, this account can help each of us face death without fear.

"While under anesthesia I had a rather unusual out-of-body experience. I knew beyond a shadow of a doubt that I was ancient, in terms of time; I had existed for thousands and thousands of years. I use the word 'time' cautiously, because time, as we understand it—past, present, and future—does not exist in that state. During this out-of-body experience there was no sense of 'time passing.' There was only the present.

"I was also aware of an expanded consciousness far superior to that which had been mine during my earthly existence. I seemed to be 'all-wise.' I realized, too, that I was neither male nor female, but both. The real me was outside the body, observing my birth into this dimension.

"I feel that this out-of-body experience has been a very important turning point in my life. Through it, as the awareness of the oneness of life has grown within me, I have become more compassionate and more thoughtful of others. I have realized that I truly am a part of that great 'I am that I am'—God!'' _C. F._

The final story is a fitting conclusion to our exploration of life on the other side. It has several features in common with the preceding stories, including descriptions of a growth in understanding, wise and supportive beings, and the feeling of timelessness. The account begins with an intriguing interaction between the nonphysical and the physical dimensions. It then takes us to a borderland and from beyond there to a hall of learning, a place of great beauty and light.

A GLIMPSE OF HEAVEN

Perhaps the most striking feature of this story is the vivid sense of God's love with which our out-of-body traveler was left. This feeling has endured after our narrator's return to the physical, where it has given rise to increased faith and the determination to help others. Simply reading this account may very well inspire you with some of that same feeling.

"I was admitted to the hospital a week before my gall-bladder operation. During this period of examination and preparation, I was resting, taking time to read my Bible and other spiritual material. It was a good opportunity to get in some meditation and prayer while I was quiet.

"One morning I was sitting up in bed, just waiting for the doctors to make their daily rounds. I began to see movement on the wall at the end of my bed, at about the level of my forehead. I remained very still. Figures of people were beckoning me to come with them. Two of them approached me and began to pull at my hands. I felt a slip as though I were moving out through my fingertips, which was followed by a thud. I was out of my body.

"I looked back at myself sitting in bed, and I had no desire to return. I saw the doctor, his assistant, and the head nurse at my bedside. The doctor was having trouble getting a pulse; the nurse said it was usually low and they sometimes had a problem finding it. I believe they were unaware that I had left my body.

"Then I was meeting with the people who had come to me. One of them who had pulled my hands was my first·cousin. I told her that I didn't know she had died. She said that she hadn't: just like me, she was over there even though she was not dead. She added, however, that she soon would be. (In fact, my cousin passed on over a year later. Since she had been ill much of her life, it was not surprising when she died at the age of forty-eight.)

"The rest of the beings who greeted me were people I didn't know in this life, but they seemed to know me from another time. Others whom I saw were deceased relatives. One of these souls was my mother, but she just kept moving along, seemingly unaware of me.

"The people I was with then took me to a place considered a border area. Some of the individuals here were sleeping. Others, finding themselves in this new place, were being told they had passed into life on the other side. Some who were there had expected to be with their God when their physical lives came to an end. Others hadn't had any idea what they expected.

"At this point I was joined by another person, whose face I did not see. I just knew he was a special guide for me. We seemed to be communicating on an inner level. The two of us walked side-by-side down a path of light until we arrived at a hall of learning.

"The beings here wore gray habits similar to those of monks. They were, however, ordinary souls earnestly seeking to know more about God and their journey to become one with Him. They had so much to learn and were so engrossed in their purpose of advancement that they were unaware of those who entered the school of higher learning.

"The school had marble pillars and a room at the end, which we entered. In the room there was a long table, with three beings seated at the center of its far side. They were neither male nor female, but a combination of both. They, too, wore habits. The one in the middle seemed to have the greatest authority.

"My guide walked to the table and handed the one on the left a scroll. The scroll, which contained my life history on earth, was passed among the three. Then the being in the center crossed out the chronicle of my life. I had neither gained nor lost. My record was now a blank and I could start over again.

"This was a judgment. With it, instant understanding passed among us, and my whole life was shown to me; I saw that which had pleased God and that which had offended Him. I was then instructed in how to conduct my life and given examples by which I could judge. There were no ifs, buts, or maybes. In these lessons I felt no sense of punishment—simply guidance in what God wanted me to do. My instruction enlightened me as to God's laws and how He judges things. I was greatly surprised. Man looks on the outward, but God looks on the heart.

"I found that I truly wanted to recognize the will of God in my life. So that I might know what He would have me do, His laws of love, grace, karma, and abundance were explained to me, and many things were brought to my remembrance.

"I was then told that I would receive help in overcoming my greatest offense against God—my negative attitude. I was assured of being in His grace for a total of three years. Then there would be a gradual return to the ordinary in life.

"My entire journey out-of-my-body was a beautiful, spiritual experience. I did not see God, but I believe the One who was at my side was Jesus.

"I still remember the laws that were given me, and I know now that the reason I'm here is to do everything possible to help others. God will take care of my needs, and He will have His way with me! There is so much I cannot write, for words fail me when I try to express His love and His laws as I experienced them."   *M. N.*

There are several messages from this final story—and from all the accounts that were so graciously sent by my correspondents over the years. These few key ideas are the ones that Edgar Cayce over and over came back to, both in his personal discussions and his psychic readings. They are the essence of what I have come to believe from nearly fifty years of exploration.

First, not only is the afterlife a certainty, but the veil between physical and nonphysical life is not as impenetrable as many people have thought.

Second, life, learning, and growth are just as much a part of our experience in the hereafter as they are while we are in material life.

Finally, God's infinite, healing love is always available to us, whether we are here on the earth or in the spirit world. The continuity of life is a gift from our loving Father-Mother. Most important, God's creation is an orderly, purposeful universe—a universe in which the Law of Love is supreme.